MW01265014

GLOBAL
CONNECTIONS

AMERICA'S ROLE IN A CHANGING WORLD

GL🌐BAL C🌐NNECTI🌐NS

GLOBAL CONNECTIONS

AMERICA'S ROLE IN A CHANGING WORLD

DOUGLAS A. PHILLIPS
SERIES EDITOR: CHARLES F. GRITZNER

CHELSEA HOUSE
PUBLISHERS
An imprint of Infobase Publishing

This book is lovingly dedicated to my children, Christopher Phillips, Angela Burnett, and Daniel Phillips. Their character and individual roles in America make the nation's future even brighter.

America's Role in a Changing World

Copyright © 2010 by Infobase Publishing

All rights reserved. No part of this book may be reproduced or utilized in any form or by any means, electronic or mechanical, including photocopying, recording, or by any information storage or retrieval systems, without permission in writing from the publisher. For information contact:

Chelsea House
An imprint of Infobase Publishing
132 West 31st Street
New York, NY 10001

Library of Congress Cataloging-in-Publication Data
Phillips, Douglas A.
  America's role in a changing world / by Douglas A. Phillips.
    p. cm. — (Global connections)
  Includes bibliographical references and index.
  ISBN 978-1-60413-287-8 (hardcover)
  1. United States—History—Juvenile literature. 2. United States—Foreign relations—Juvenile literature. 3. National characteristics, American—Juvenile literature. 4. World politics—Juvenile literature. I. Title.
  E178.3.P55 2009
  973—dc22
                                        2008054881

Chelsea House books are available at special discounts when purchased in bulk quantities for businesses, associations, institutions, or sales promotions. Please call our Special Sales Department in New York at (212) 967-8800 or (800) 322-8755.

You can find Chelsea House on the World Wide Web
at http://www.chelseahouse.com

Text design by Annie O'Donnell
Cover design by Takeshi Takahashi
Composition by EJB Publishing Services
Cover printed by Bang Printing, Brainerd, MN
Book printed and bound by Bang Printing, Brainerd, MN
Date printed: March 2010
Printed in the United States of America

10 9 8 7 6 5 4 3 2 1

This book is printed on acid-free paper.

All links and Web addresses were checked and verified to be correct at the time of publication. Because of the dynamic nature of the Web, some addresses and links may have changed since publication and may no longer be valid.

CONTENTS

INTRODUCTION

A GLOBAL COMMUNITY

Globalization is the process of coming together as a closely connected global community. It began thousands of years ago, when tribal groups and small hunting parties wandered from place to place. The process accelerated following Columbus's epic voyage more than five centuries ago. Europeans—an estimated 50 million of them—spread out to occupy lands throughout the world. This migration transformed the distribution of the world's peoples and their cultures forever. In the United States and Canada, for example, most people speak a West European language. Most practice a religious faith with roots in the ancient Middle East and eat foods originating in Asia.

Today, we are citizens of a closely interwoven global community. Events occurring half a world away can be watched and experienced, often as they happen, in our own homes. People, materials, and even diseases can be transported from continent to continent in a single day, thanks to jet planes. Electronic communications make possible the instantaneous exchange of information by phone, e-mail, or other means with friends or business associates almost anywhere in the world. Trade and commerce, perhaps more so than any other aspect of our daily lives, amply illustrate the importance of global linkages. How many things in your home (including your clothing) are of international origin? What foods and beverages have you consumed today that came from other lands? Could Northern America's economy survive without foreign oil, iron ore, copper, or other vital resources?

The GLOBAL CONNECTIONS series is designed to help you realize how closely people and places are tied to one another within the expanding global community. Each book introduces you to political, economic, environmental, social, medical, and other timely issues, problems, and prospects. The authors and editors hope you enjoy and learn from these books. May they hand you a passport to intellectual travels throughout our fascinating, complex, and increasingly "intradependent" world!

—*Charles F. Gritzner*
Series Editor

THE WORLD'S MOST POWERFUL NATION

In its relatively short history, the United States of America has become a superpower beyond all others, but today the country faces many challenges. Bank failures, the closing of major industries, rising unemployment, and the threat of terrorist attacks present both challenge and opportunity. The country's role in the world is changing in both predictable and unforeseen ways.

The story of the United States is not one of steady growth and opportunity. Its past has been marked by many problems and setbacks. The present and future also hold tremendous opportunities, as the country has a history of rising to meet new challenges. At the heart of this book lies the essential question: Who, exactly, is the United States and how is its role in the world changing?

With the world's largest economy and strongest military, the United States was in an unchallenged position of superiority at the end of the twentieth century. Even with the vicious terrorist attacks by al Qaeda on September 11, 2001, the United States recovered. It vigorously pursued the terrorists, and the U.S. economy expanded to reach new levels. While the country remained the world's top military and economic power at the end of the first decade of the twenty-first century, other nations appear ready to compete. China and Russia are increasing in both economic and military power. While Japan's economy represents the world's second-highest gross domestic product (GDP), China may soon surpass it. Plus, with 1.3 billion people, China may soon rise farther to surpass the United States' economic position. The Asian powerhouse is also increasing its military and space exploration efforts. Thus, the United States faces many obstacles in the decades ahead in its challenge to remain the world's greatest superpower.

THE RISE TO POWER

The United States has evolved from early settlements and a collection of colonies to the position of global superpower that it holds today. How has this happened? A wide variety of causes that detail the country's path to greatness will be explored in this book. The land and the people represent vital elements in this story. So, however, do many other factors. The country's government structure, cultural diversity, and even strokes of good luck have also contributed. For example, the United States is located on a continent and hemisphere that lacks other powerful competing countries. This bit of luck has greatly benefited the country. It has not had to fight constantly to defend itself against aggressive neighbors. The Atlantic and Pacific oceans have also provided a buffer that has often protected the United States from outside powers.

THE UNITED STATES' GLOBAL IMPACT

With its tremendous economic, cultural, military, and political power, the United States exerts a huge impact on other countries and their people. The U.S. military has served in many places

UNITED STATES: SUPERPOWER

The chant of "We're number one!" resonates around sports events as teams and their fans claim supremacy. The United States, a twentieth- and twenty-first-century superpower, can also claim a number of categories in which it leads the world. Among them are the following:

- Best universities (Harvard tops the list)
- Most university students
- Economic competitiveness
- Labor market efficiency
- Innovation
- Most Olympic medals
- Most popular Web sites (Yahoo, Google, YouTube)
- Highest obesity rate
- World's most profitable company (ExxonMobile)
- Most Nobel Prize winners
- Largest Christian population
- Highest electrical consumption
- Most airports
- Most computers

Some of these categories, such as being the world's leader in obesity, are nothing to brag about. In addition, the United States does *not* lead the world in other notable categories, including percentage of citizens with health care (ranked 19th), life expectancy (46th), per capita GDP (10th), and education expenditures as a percentage of GDP (57th). Even with a variety of problem areas, the United States leads or is near the top in a large number of categories, providing further evidence that the United States is a superpower. Watch for other U.S. rankings as you read through this book and those you find in other sources.

During its decades as a superpower, America has made its mark economically, militarily, culturally, and politically. Evidence of the country's influence can be seen around the world in unusual places, such as this McDonald's outlet in Kuala Lumpur, Malaysia.

around the world. Today, troops are stationed in many lands, including Japan, Germany, Iraq, Afghanistan, and South Korea. Military personnel also serve in most countries around the world as military attachés stationed at American embassies. The strength of the U.S. military serves as a warning: Might causes fright for potential enemies. The U.S. position was presented in a stern warning provided by President Theodore Roosevelt more than a century ago. Roosevelt stated that the United States should "speak softly and carry a big stick." His words sent a clear message that if diplomacy fails, the United States is prepared to act militarily.

Politically, the United States has major roles in the world. The country provides large amounts of foreign aid to needy nations. It also speaks with a powerful voice for democracy and human rights. The country has a veto in the United Nations and is an important member in many international organizations. The political and military roles of the United States will be explained further in Chapter 7.

The United States' culture and economy reach around the world and into the daily lives of billions of people. From the soft drinks and fast food consumed, to music and television programs, American popular culture is on display. Today, it is found almost everywhere and plays an important part in the lives of people around the world. The United States' huge cultural reach is discussed in more detail in Chapter 8.

The global impact of the U.S. economy was clearly demonstrated in 2008 when the country's housing market problem spread around the world. Huge losses in the U.S. stock market crashed upon the shores of Asia and Europe in a matter of hours. Echoes of stock and bond losses reverberated around the planet as banks failed and some countries teetered on the brink of bankruptcy. While the primary cause of the crisis came from the housing loans in the United States, solutions to this problem also first came from the United States. Thus, in an economically connected world, the United States plays the primary role in the world's economy. Chapter 6 expands upon the country's economic role.

SEARCH FOR A MORE PERFECT UNION

Even as the world's superpower, the United States has held firmly to the belief of working to create a more perfect union. This statement comes from the preamble to the U.S. Constitution, which is the primary document establishing the U.S. government. In working to create a more perfect union, the country continues a centuries-old quest to provide equality, freedom, justice, and economic opportunity to its citizens. History shows that the

MAKING CONNECTIONS

HOW DO YOU CONNECT TO THE WORLD?

Our daily life is tremendously impacted by connections from around the world. Much of the food we eat, the clothes we wear, and the cars we drive come from elsewhere. So does much of our energy and other essential natural resources. Make a list of the countries with which you come in contact during a single day. Things to look for can include the following:

- Clothing, foods and beverages, transportation
- Television, radios, CD players, and other media-related devices; games and entertainment
- Local immigrants and new U.S. citizens
- Small and large appliances

What do your findings reveal about how tightly linked the world is today?

process has been slow. The benefits of greater equality, justice, and economic opportunities, for example, have not always been equally enjoyed by women and minorities. However, the continuing pursuit of excellence and a more perfect union strengthens the United States' efforts to stride forward for all of its citizens.

WHAT IS AHEAD

The United States has changed over time, but so, too, has most of the world. Some nineteenth-century powers are fading, while new countries are rising. India and China have made major advances on the world's stage. These two countries, alone, account for about 36 percent of the world's population. New nuclear powers have emerged. Pakistan and North Korea now possess nuclear weapons, and Iran is working to develop the technology. Global terrorism has gripped the twenty-first century after the horrendous attacks on the United States in 2001. These heartless acts affected not only the United States, but also other countries around the world.

The closely intertwined global economy has also taken on immense complexity. Human rights, economic inequality, sexism, and racism have become major global issues that confront a world that is still led by the United States. Other global issues are ethnic cleansing, war, pollution, energy, and the impacts of possible climate change. The 2008 U.S. presidential election between senators Barack Obama and John McCain signaled new directions for the country and its place in the world. The journey through these chapters will help readers to better understand the United States' roles in a changing world.

AMERICA'S CLIMB TO THE TOP

The rise of the United States is a remarkable story of advancement. From a ragtag bunch of colonies, the country has risen to unparalleled levels of power and success. How has this happened? In this chapter and the next, we'll explore the highlights of the United States' path to power through the nineteenth century.

The Americas were once lands inhabited by Native Americans. These peoples proudly held the lands in the Americas, until they encountered the European powers that possessed superior technology. The Europeans were seeking to stretch their reach, economic influence, and cultures across the world during the fifteenth through nineteenth centuries. The Americas quickly became an area of interest because of the vast land area and potential riches.

COLONIES FIGHT FOR FREEDOM

In North America the European powers included the Spanish, French, Swedish, Dutch, and the British. Most of these powers established colonies and pushed Native Americans off their lands. The British soon dominated the East Coast areas of the future United States. Americans supported the British in their global struggles for an empire against the French and others. However, as the American colonies matured, they sought and fought for greater independence from the British. They would also soon reach out to develop relationships with other countries. With the embryo cast by the Declaration of Independence in 1776, the United States of America had started its journey toward becoming a world power.

After the Europeans arrived, the United States became a land of thirteen colonies. By the early 1700s, the British controlled the colonies that later became states in the United States. Resentment against outside rule grew steadily during the 1770s. In April 1776, a rebellion started, with the first shots fired at Lexington and Concord in Massachusetts. From this small initial rebel effort, the rise of the United States began. In June 1775, George Washington was appointed commander of the Continental army by the recently convened Continental Congress. The fledgling Continental army was greatly undermanned and poorly trained. It was also undisciplined and underfinanced compared to the British forces, which were considered to be the best in the world. Washington's job was to take the ragtag mix of farmers and other patriots and turn them into an effective fighting force.

The British controlled the seas, a lesson that the United States learned and would apply later in its history. British forces won most of the early land battles. However, the Americans won an important victory at Saratoga (New York). It enticed the French, traditional enemies of the British, to become allies and trading partners of the Americans. This factor later proved to be the turning point of the Revolutionary War, even though the United States struggled on the battlefields through the 1770s. In 1781, the American forces and their French allies cornered the British at Yorktown (Virginia) and won a stunning victory. Some fighting took place after Yorktown, but the Peace of Paris between the British and Americans was signed on September 10, 1783. Relations remained tense between the British and Americans, but most of the fighting had ended. The unlikely U.S. victory was greatly aided by the French, and the new nation had survived its difficult birth.

FORGING A NEW GOVERNMENT

After freeing themselves from British control, the next major problem facing the Americans was an ineffective central government. The Articles of Confederation were ratified in 1781 but quickly proved to be inadequate. A major weakness was the lack of a strong central government. This meant that states were each able to create their own currency and taxes. The central national government had no control over these matters. The national government had to ask the states for money, a very ineffective process that left the army underpaid and undersupplied. In the absence of a strong central government that could intervene, squabbles between states also arose and festered. Thus, in 1787, the states sent representatives to Philadelphia to come up with a better way to govern themselves.

The Constitutional Convention established a new constitution that was widely debated and discussed. Disagreements flourished as many feared the creation of a strong national government that did not protect the rights of individuals. Only 9 states were required to ratify the new constitution, but problems would exist if major states like New York or Virginia did not ratify the document. Finally, after two and a half years, all 13 of the original states ratified the U.S. Constitution. This was a significant development. This marvelous document has been the key to political stability that has helped the United States to become a world power.

Even though the United States and Great Britain had signed a peace treaty after the Revolutionary War, the relationship was still unstable. The British continued to meddle in U.S. affairs.

For example, they disrupted U.S. trade with France, their global enemy. They believed that this trade aided the French, against whom they were fighting in the Napoleonic Wars in Europe. The British navy also captured many American sailors. More than 10,000 of them were taken off U.S. ships and forced to work on British naval vessels. Some historians also believe that the United States was hoping to take Canada from the British, since they were occupied elsewhere fighting against the French. Thus, the trade problems, capture of sailors, and Canadian possibilities led the United States to declare war on the British. This was the start of the War of 1812.

Both countries were inadequately prepared to fight the War of 1812. The British were tied down by battles against the French,

When the Founding Fathers met to draw up the U.S. Constitution, few would have imagined that their "more perfect union" would one day be the world's greatest superpower.

led by Napoleon, in Europe. The United States had problems organizing and financing an army to fight the war. The war was fought to a stalemate over the next two years, with both sides growing weary of the fighting. Both paid dearly for the fighting as their national debts ballooned. The British wanted to complete their victory in Europe and reestablish trade with the United States. The United States wanted to end the British blockades, which had nearly shut down trade. The war-torn country also needed repairs, including to Washington, D.C., which the British had burned in 1814. Even the White House, home to the president, was burned during the war. Both sides agreed to end the fighting with the Treaty of Ghent (Belgium), which was signed in 1815. Neither side gained or lost significant land areas in the war settlement. However, this treaty marked a major transition in the relationship between the two countries. The British and Americans took steps toward becoming key allies and trading partners. This vital relationship has lasted two centuries.

THE UNITED STATES GROWS LARGER

After independence, the United States looked westward and northward in terms of growth. Native Americans still occupied many lands to the west, but the French had seized control of these lands during the eighteenth century. The United States had made an attempt to take Canada from the British, but that dream failed with the end of the War of 1812. Hungry for growth and new land areas, the United States embarked on efforts to increase the country's size. Nineteenth-century land gains greatly expanded the area and strength of the country. They provided the land and resource base that has proved to be a key factor in the country's rise to that of a world power. What were these new land acquisitions and how were they obtained?

A major land acquisition took place in 1803. This area was called the Louisiana Purchase, which the United States obtained from France for $23 million. With the Louisiana Purchase, the United States grew in area by 828,000 square miles (2,140,000 square kilometers). This territory gained included all or part of the following states: Arkansas, Iowa, Missouri, Kansas, Oklahoma, Minnesota, South Dakota, North Dakota, Nebraska, Kansas, New Mexico, Texas, Montana, Wyoming, Colorado, and, of course, Louisiana. The French were willing to part with this land because they were on the brink of war with the British in Europe. The United States was pleased with the land gains. Of great importance was the fact that a major world power was moved away from bordering the United States. Without the French nearby, the United States became the dominant regional power in North America.

MAKING CONNECTIONS

KEY FACTORS IN THE UNITED STATES' RISE

The amazing journey of the United States from the colonial era to the end of the nineteenth century took the country from a ragtag set of colonies to a regional power. How did this happen? Reflect upon the following questions and research further to understand the incredible story of the United States from its independence to 1898 and the Spanish-American War.

- ➡ What key things did the new U.S. nation do to consolidate power and become effective after independence?
- ➡ What internal factors do you believe were the most important in building the United States as a regional power?
- ➡ What external factors do you believe were the most important in building the United States as a regional power?
- ➡ How has the idea of isolationism affected the United States' role in the world?

The United States grew again in 1845 when the Republic of Texas joined the Union. Between 1836 and 1845, Texas was an independent country that existed between Mexico and the United States. Texas had seceded from Mexico and was annexed (claimed) by the United States in 1845 with a vote in Texas that agreed to the annexation. Texas agreed to this with the understanding that the U.S. government would assume all of its debts. Further, Texas and its large Anglo population sought protection from Mexico. This fear was soon realized, and the United States defeated Mexico only three years later in the Mexican-American War of 1848.

The Treaty of Guadalupe Hidalgo ended the Mexican-American War. With the treaty, the United States gained a huge area of land that included all of California, Nevada, and Utah. It also obtained parts of New Mexico, Arizona, Colorado, and Wyoming. In contrast, Mexico lost nearly a third of its land area with the treaty. Additional parts of Arizona and New Mexico were ceded (surrendered) by Mexico to the United States in 1853. This land acquisition was the Gadsden Purchase, for which the United States paid $10 million.

The United States also expanded its border and removed another world power from the continent when it purchased Alaska from Russia in 1867. The purchase was dubbed Seward's Folly or Seward's Icebox because many people thought the land was useless. William Seward was the U.S. secretary of state who promoted the purchase. The United States paid $7.2 million for Alaska, which amounts to 1.9 cents per acre. Today, the state contributes more than its original purchase price to the U.S. economy each day!

The last major piece of the United States' land puzzle came when Hawaii was annexed in 1898. Hawaii, like Texas, was formerly an independent country. The United States had even recognized the Kingdom of Hawaii in 1842. Many business people celebrated Hawaii's annexation, but many local indigenous people were saddened by the land grab. This was also true of Alaska, as both states still have very small factions that support independence from the United States.

While the eighteenth century saw the United States become independent and establish a government, the nineteenth century saw the country greatly expand its land area. The new land areas provided the United States with a huge resource base that could be utilized for business and government. In addition, the country had removed two major powers, France and Russia, from North America. Thus, by the end of the nineteenth century, North and South America had a new major power in the neighborhood—the United States of America.

THE UNITED STATES BECOMES A REGIONAL POWER

The nineteenth century ended with the land area of the United States being much as it is today. From the East Coast hearth, the country now stretched from the Atlantic Ocean into the Pacific and northward beyond the Arctic Circle. But U.S. power had also grown beyond its borders. The country had an isolationist policy until its ships began to be attacked by pirates along North Africa's Barbary Coast. Long observant of the British, Americans understood the importance of sea power. Thus, the country used its fledgling navy to win the First Barbary War (1801–1806). This victory established that the young nation could conduct and win a naval war in faraway lands.

U.S. dominance in North and South America continued to grow throughout the nineteenth century. Other major world powers had left the continents or had lost most of their influence in the Americas. Therefore, the playing field was wide open for the United States to stretch its reach and grow as a regional power in North and South America.

The Monroe Doctrine

Many Spanish colonies in the Americas became independent in the early nineteenth century. The United States had a national security interest in keeping the influence of European powers out of the Americas. To achieve this goal, U.S. president James

Monroe drew a stern "line in the sand." In 1823, in what has come to be known as the Monroe Doctrine, he stated that European powers were no longer welcome to colonize or interfere with the new countries in the Americas. With the support of the British, the United States had declared its interest in protecting the Americas from European interests. The Monroe Doctrine served as a warning to the Russians, French, Spanish, and oth-

AMERICAN DOCTRINES

The United States has had a number of foreign policy doctrines in its history. A doctrine is a rule or principle that establishes a country's important foreign policy stands. In the case of the United States, it sets forth a warning to other countries. In addition to the Monroe Doctrine of 1823, there are other key U.S. foreign policy doctrines. Here are a few of the doctrines and the year they were proclaimed:

- **Roosevelt Corollary to the Monroe Doctrine (1904)** President Theodore Roosevelt amended the Monroe Doctrine by stating that the United States had the right to intervene to stabilize the economy of Central American and Caribbean nations.
- **The Truman Doctrine (1947)** President Harry Truman promised that the United States would supply aid to Greece and Turkey after World War II to keep them from falling under the Communist control of the Soviet Union. This was one of the early attempts, called containment, to stop the spread of Communism.
- **The Eisenhower Doctrine (1957)** President Dwight Eisenhower proclaimed that the United States would use armed forces in response to imminent or actual foreign aggression. He further promised that nations opposing Communism would receive aid.

ers that they were to stay out of independent countries in the Americas.

In 1854, the United States reached across the Pacific to stretch its influence. Japan had long been closed to most outsiders, but this changed when U.S. naval commodore Matthew Perry sailed for the second time into Tokyo Bay. With the United States posing a huge military threat, Japan, under duress, signed the

> ➲ **The Nixon Doctrine (1969)** President Richard Nixon affirmed existing treaty commitments and the continued nuclear shield of the United States for allies. However, he also stated that other nations would be responsible for their own military defense.
> ➲ **The Carter Doctrine (1980)** President Jimmy Carter stated that the United States would use military force to protect interests in the Persian Gulf. This was offered as a clear message to the Soviet Union, which had invaded Afghanistan in 1979.
> ➲ **Reagan Corollary to the Carter Doctrine (1981)** President Ronald Reagan extended the Carter Doctrine by stating that the United States would step in, if needed, to protect Saudi Arabia, a key U.S. ally and oil supplier. The doctrine was implemented because of the threat of the Iraq and Iran War (1980–1988) spilling over to Saudi Arabia and threatening the interests of the United States.
> ➲ **The Bush Doctrine (2002)** Created in the wake of the attacks of September 11, 2001, President George W. Bush stated that the United States would treat nations that harbor or assist terrorists like terrorists. This doctrine was employed to invade Afghanistan in 2001 and Iraq in 2003.

This political cartoon illustrates the Monroe Doctrine, the 1823 declaration intended to protect the Americas from European interests. The cartoon shows a bayonet-wielding Uncle Sam defending Nicaragua and Venezuela from several incredulous European nations.

Convention of Kanagawa. This unequal treaty greatly favored the United States by opening Japanese ports to trade, protecting U.S. sailors, and having an American consul in Japan. More importantly, it was a preface to the use of U.S. military power in more distant locations as a growing world power.

The Civil War

Fortunes of the United States took a very dark turn with the devastating Civil War, a conflict that lasted from 1861 to 1865. Primarily fought over the issue of slavery, the United States survived with the leadership of President Abraham Lincoln and superior military forces. The country, however, took a huge backward step in economic development. Much of the South lay in ruins and disarray. The decade after the Civil War was spent reconstructing the United States and expanding civil rights for former slaves.

During the Civil War, the North was wary of European powers who wanted to meddle in the war by supporting the South. With a fleet three times larger than the Confederacy (the South), Lincoln used a blockade of Confederate ports in 1861 to prevent other nations from supporting the South's economy. The blockade shut down the South's vital cotton trade. However, the British attempted to work around these blockades from various Caribbean colonies. When the Union (Northern forces) caught such ships, they would give the seized goods to their own sailors. The Confederacy tried to strike back with its own naval forces. With an enemy that possessed superior numbers of ships, the South used technology to try to address its numerical shortcomings. The Confederacy had some new ideas that included ironclad ships like the CSS *Virginia*, which is better known as the *Merrimack*. The use of ironclad vessels made wooden ships inferior for fighting. But the Union copied the *Merrimack*'s design and countered with its own ironclad vessel, the USS *Monitor*. The Confederacy also used submarines, mines, and torpedo boats to attack Union ships. These ideas would also serve to advance the U.S. Navy after the war.

Manifest Destiny

The balance of the nineteenth century continued the development of the western United States as the idea of Manifest Destiny came to fruition. Manifest Destiny was the nineteenth-century belief that the United States had a destiny of stretching from the Atlantic Ocean to the Pacific Ocean and beyond. This philosophy was behind the United States' hunger to acquire the lands previously mentioned in this chapter.

In addition to Manifest Destiny, Americans enjoyed economic growth and prosperity in the waning decades of the nineteenth century. Westward movement and settlement served to develop the nation's economy. Rail transportation and the telegraph stretched new lines across the West, as the country built an infrastructure for economic activity. Some domestic conflicts were being resolved with Native Americans by treaty, but others were concluded by force and other unsavory means.

AMERICA EMERGES AS A WORLD POWER

The twentieth century belonged to the United States. The country had risen from a regional power to a position of global preeminence. But the United States faced intense hurdles and would soon be severely challenged and sorely tested. World Wars I and II and the Cold War were much different and much larger conflicts than the country had faced previously. In each of these wars, the United States played a key role in creating and preserving democratic societies across the world. In addition, the country's economy grew to become the world's largest. This economic machine fueled the nation's military power. Combined, they thrust the country into the role of a superpower by the end of the twentieth century—the United States' century.

At the end of the nineteenth century, the United States was a regional power on the brink of going global. The country's entrance on the world's power stage actually started in 1898, two years before the new century. Why is this date important in U.S.

history? What event served to propel the United States forward into the new century as a world power?

THE SPANISH-AMERICAN WAR

An earthshaking event took place in 1898 when the United States defeated Spain in the Spanish-American War. The United States had effectively removed Spain, a traditional colonial power, from the Americas. The war started as the United States accused Spain of sinking the USS *Maine* in the harbor at Havana, Cuba. Spain claimed that the sinking was caused by an internal explosion. The United States said it was a Spanish mine. In any case, 266 American men died, and the fuse was lit for war. Journalists and citizens in the United States clamored for war with the cry of "Remember the Maine, to Hell with Spain."

The war started in April 1898, and the first battle was fought far from Cuba, in the Spanish colony of the Philippines. Commodore George Dewey led the U.S. Navy to a quick victory on May 1, 1898, and soon after, the Philippines declared their independence. However, conflicts between the United States and Spain still remained.

One battle turned out to be a comedy. Captain Henry Glass of the USS *Charleston* was ordered to take the small island of Guam. Upon arrival, he fired his ship's cannons at the island's fortification. The Spanish officers on Guam did not know that war had been declared and thought that the cannon fire was a salute greeting. Thus, they sailed out to the *Charleston* to ask for gunpowder so that they could return the greeting salute to the ship. The Spanish officers were captured, and Guam was taken by the United States with little effort.

Cuba was taken with forces including the Rough Riders, which had Lieutenant Colonel Theodore Roosevelt, the future president, as second-in-command. The final victory for the United States was at Santiago, Cuba, where 24,000 Spanish troops surrendered. Shortly afterward, the United States seized Puerto Rico.

Fighting stopped on August 12, 1898, and the Treaty of Paris finalized the provisions that ended the Spanish-American War. The United States had fought successful battles in many locations around the world. And it had won an incredible victory. As a result, Spain ceded (surrendered) Guam and Puerto Rico to the United States and received $20 million in compensation. In addition, Spain removed its troops from Cuba and essentially was out of the Americas. The United States was now poised on the world's stage as a military power to be reckoned with. Larger challenges, however, loomed ahead.

WORLD WAR I (1914–1918)

Expansion of the United States' global interests was furthered in 1900. This occurred when Congress passed the Open Door Policy that required China to provide equal trading opportunities to all countries. While the policy showed the country's interests in Asia, the strategy later became dormant when Japan invaded Manchuria, China, in 1941.

During the second decade of the twentieth century, ominous clouds began to form over Europe. The storm clouds burst after the assassination of Archduke Franz Ferdinand in Sarajevo (a city located today in Bosnia and Herzegovina) in 1914. Ferdinand was heir to the throne of the Austro-Hungarian Empire. This event triggered a chain reaction that quickly spread across Europe. Soon, the Entente Powers (also referred to as the Allies) of the United Kingdom, France, and Russia were engaged in an immense war against the Central Powers of Germany and Austria-Hungary. Other nations were quickly drawn into the conflict, which had spread to Africa, Asia, and the Pacific by the end of 1914.

The United States and some other nations chose to remain neutral and isolationist during the early phases of World War I. U.S. attempts were made to promote peace, but these failed. When the British cruise ship the *Lusitania* was sunk by a German U-boat, 128 Americans were aboard the vessel. The United

States protested to Germany that cruise ships should not be attacked, and Germany agreed. In 1917, however, Germany went back on its agreement and allowed its submarines to attack ships without restrictions. This, combined with other events, including the Zimmerman Telegram, led the United States into the war.

The Zimmerman Telegram was a message sent from the German foreign secretary to the German ambassador in the United States. This note was intercepted by the British, who shared it with the United States. The note told of the Germans' interest in having Mexico declare war against the United States if the United States entered the war as an ally of Britain, France, and Russia. In return, Mexico was to be offered the states it had lost in the Mexican-American War.

The United States Enters the War

The United States was furious about the unrestricted German submarine warfare and the scenario posed by the Zimmerman Telegram. President Woodrow Wilson asked Congress to declare war on Germany. On April 6, 1917, the body passed the declaration of war. The United States was now formally engaged in World War I. By the summer of 1918, 4 million American men had been drafted into the military. Most were sent to France to fight the Germans, who had occupied the country. Soon, the tide turned against the Germans as the strength of the Allies pushed Germany back from its summer offensive. By the fall of 1918, the Allies had won a crushing victory. However, the casualties had been immense. Twenty million people had died, about 120,000 of whom were Americans. Millions of others were left with lifelong injuries. Infrastructure was ruined across the continent of Europe. Some countries disappeared, and new ones were born. In another sense, the United States was reborn again as a recognized world power. The U.S. military had helped the Allies defeat a powerful enemy. The war formally ended with the signing of the Treaty of Versailles in June 1919.

President Wilson's Fourteen Points

In 1918, President Wilson sought to influence the future direction that both the United States and the world would take. His ideas were presented in a "Fourteen Points" speech he delivered to Congress. The points included many important ideas for peace, including the following four:

- Open diplomacy and peace agreements (secret agreements had led to the rapid spread of countries involved in World War I)
- Freedom of navigation on the seas
- Equality of trade and removal of trade barriers
- The need to create an association of nations

While the British, the French, and even the U.S. Congress opposed some of Wilson's ideas, the League of Nations was created in 1919 after Wilson's first call for an association of nations. Ironically, the United States did not join the League of Nations. Senate Republicans blocked the measure because they believed that the United States should remain isolationist. Thus, the United States did not ratify the treaty and never joined the League of Nations. President Wilson, however, did receive the Nobel Peace Prize in 1920 for his efforts to promote peace and understanding between countries.

Lingering Issues After World War I

After World War I, the United States was firmly entrenched as a world power. But the country still had a bit of a split personality. While it had proven itself as a military and economic power during World War I, it still displayed strong isolationist tendencies. The desire to avoid foreign entanglements remained strong after President Wilson left office. The economy grew stronger until 1929. In that year, the stock market crashed and plunged the country into the Great Depression.

On the international front, the United States saw a new tide rising in Russia. The Communists (Bolsheviks) had seized power from Tsar Nicholas II in 1917. At the time, Russia was weary from World War I and faced domestic problems. Vladimir Lenin led the October Revolution against the tsar and used the writings of Karl Marx to develop an ideology called Marxism-Leninism. Today, this political ideology is commonly called Communism. The Russian Revolution initiated the spread of this philosophy. The United States viewed this development with concern. There were many in the United States who feared that the "red tide" of the Communist Revolution could spread to the United States.

WORLD WAR II (1939–1945)

By the late 1930s, the United States and the world were slowly emerging from the Great Depression. But new problems arose on the global horizon. One involved Japan. The island nation had greatly increased its military strength and was using its power to conquer new lands in Asia. Japan invaded and seized Manchuria in 1931 and mounted a full-scale invasion of China in 1937. This initiated the intrusion of Japanese forces into Asia and the Pacific region in search of natural resources and regional control.

In Europe, a reborn Germany, led by Adolf Hitler, defied other European powers and the conditions agreed upon in the Treaty of Versailles and rearmed. It used its new military power in the Rhineland in 1936 in defiance of the Treaty of Versailles, the peace treaty signed by Germany and the Allied powers at the end of World War I. Also, in 1935, Italy invaded Ethiopia. Seeking partners for his future plans, Hitler formed an alliance with Italy and Japan in 1939. Italy, Germany, and Japan presented a formidable coalition called the Axis. Soon they would become bolder in their military aggression.

Germany annexed Austria in 1938 and claimed the Sudetenland in Czechoslovakia. The British and French agreed to this because Hitler promised he would not demand further lands. The promise was quickly broken as Hitler boldly moved into Poland in 1939. Finally, after the invasion of Poland, major European powers saw that Hitler was aggressively moving to establish German domination on the continent. France and the United Kingdom declared war on Germany in September 1939.

A Secret Pact

Germany invaded Poland after establishing a secret agreement with the Soviet Union. This nonaggression agreement, called the Molotov-Ribbentrop Pact, was signed in August 1939. The agreement allowed the two powers to divide Poland and other Eastern European countries between them. Sixteen days after Germany invaded Poland, the Soviet Union also invaded the country. The Soviets then moved military forces into the Baltic nations of Estonia, Latvia, and Lithuania later in 1939. In November, the Soviets invaded Finland. In April 1940, Germany attacked Denmark and Norway, and both were quickly conquered. Germany invaded France, Belgium, and the Netherlands in May. By the end of June, all three had fallen. Japan was invading areas around the Pacific and Asia. Events were rapidly spinning out of control. The United States, however, was still on the sidelines as much of the world was disintegrating.

The United States had stayed on the sidelines militarily while the war in Europe and Asia had raged from 1939 until December of 1941. The carryover of isolationist policies had kept the country out of the war. In 1941, however, the United States started providing war materials to the Allies though a lend-lease program. The United States also cut off supplies of oil and other raw materials to Japan. This was no small measure, as the United States then supplied over three-fourths of Japan's oil. The growing global crisis would not allow the United States to remain isolationist.

December 7, 1941

On December 7, 1941, the Japanese surprised U.S. forces with an unprovoked attack at Pearl Harbor, Hawaii. The event remains a scar deeply embedded in the United States' collective memory. But a statement made during the attack by Japanese admiral Isoroku Yamamoto was most prophetic. He said, "I fear we have awakened a sleeping giant." Japan had recognized that the United States was the only other Pacific Ocean power that could fend off its imperialistic intentions in the region. With the attack at Pearl Harbor, Japan hoped to knock out the United States' naval and air strength in the region. Instead, Admiral Yamamoto was right: A sleeping giant had been awakened.

On December 7, Japan had not only attacked Pearl Harbor, but also the United States' Pacific territories at Wake Island and Guam. Japan also invaded Thailand and Malaya the same day and conducted air attacks at Hong Kong, the Philippines, Singapore, and in China. Its declaration of war against the United States, also on the same day, left no doubt as to its imperialistic intentions.

President Franklin D. Roosevelt asked Congress to declare war on Japan, and the legislative body did on December 8, 1941. Germany and Italy declared war on the United States on December 11, with the United States responding in kind the same day. The next day, the United States reciprocated when Romania and Bulgaria declared war on it. Thus, in the span of five fast-paced days, the United States was at war in many faraway places around the world. The new superpower was awake!

The United States was now faced with a war on two major fronts. A decision was made to pursue the war against Germany first, while holding a defensive posture in the Pacific region. This priority was given partly because British prime minister Winston Churchill had been working to convince President Roosevelt to help protect the United Kingdom. Roosevelt was also inclined to fight Germany first, but the American public had not been convinced of the merit and wanted to stay out of the European conflict. The attack at Pearl Harbor quickly changed the view. Support for the European war galvanized quickly after December 7.

Putting Together a Military Force

As the United States geared up its industrial and military machines, the military draft was already in process. Seeing the strong potential that the United States would be engaged in World War II, Roosevelt had started a peacetime draft in September 1940. The draft selected men from the population and ordered them to report for induction into the military. Millions

Any isolationist tendencies the United States still had after World War I were shattered when Japan attacked Pearl Harbor, effectively bringing the nation into World War II. On June 6, 1944—D-Day—the United States worked with the Allied powers to assault invading Germans at Normandy (above). By the end of the war, the United States had elevated its world status.

of young American men were drafted during World War II, and their heroic efforts began to turn the tide against Germany and the other Axis nations in 1943. On June 6, 1944, known as D-Day, the United States and its allies formed the largest war assault in history as they stormed the beach at Normandy (located on the north coast of France). From their foothold in Normandy, the Allies worked to push the Germans back to their homeland and forced their surrender in 1945.

The war in the Pacific with Japan started out defensively, but the advantage turned to the United States in June 1942 with the sea battle at Midway. This naval battle lasted four days but resulted in a resounding U.S. victory after Japan had attacked Midway Atoll. Four Japanese aircraft carriers and a cruiser were sunk during the fighting. The battle at Midway changed the war in the Pacific. The former aggressor, Japan, was now forced to be on the defensive. U.S. forces began to push the Japanese out of the various lands they had conquered.

The U.S. forces island-hopped toward Japan in pursuit of Japanese forces. As the invasion loomed, the United States pondered options for forcing the surrender of Japan. One option held that the tenacious Japanese would fight furiously for their homeland and would not surrender. U.S. president Harry Truman and others feared that U.S. troop losses would be immense with an invasion. Critics feared the loss of thousands of Japanese civilians. Still, after considering all options, Truman decided to use atomic weapons in war for the first time in history. The atomic bombs used at the cities of Hiroshima and Nagasaki in August 1945 caused Japan to surrender quickly. With World War II over, the United States was universally recognized as a superpower. Its military, economic, and political power exceeded all others. However, a new challenger was rising in Eurasia.

THE COLD WAR (1945–1991)

The United States, the United Kingdom, the Soviet Union, Canada, France, Australia, and other Allies emerged victorious from

World War II. Germany emerged as a divided nation that was split between France, the United Kingdom, the United States, and the Soviet Union. The city of Berlin was also divided into four parts. Soon after, the United States, France, and the United Kingdom joined their sectors of Berlin and Germany into one. The Soviet Union, however, chose to maintain the fourth section separately. This disagreement was only one of many that emerged between the United States and the Soviet Union following the war. The Americans, British, and French feared Soviet control in Europe, especially Eastern Europe. They had seen the dishonesty and blood-soaked hands of Russian premier Joseph Stalin before, during, and after the war.

As Stalin established Communist puppet governments in countries in Eastern Europe, the United States and its allies worked to contain the Soviets and the growing threat of Communism. The fundamental differences between Communism and capitalism were major economic and philosophical divisions between the Americans and Soviets. In addition, the Soviet government was not a democracy. The country was ruled by a powerful dictatorship of elite Communist Party members.

In 1948, Stalin established a blockade in Berlin to prevent supplies and materials from arriving from the West into the Soviet sector. In response, the United States and its allies flew supplies into the city in what is known as the Berlin Airlift of 1948 and 1949. The airlift was a major embarrassment to the Soviets, who lifted the blockade in September 1949. In the same year, France, the United States, and the United Kingdom combined their three sectors to form West Germany. In response, the Soviets proclaimed their part of occupied Germany as the German Democratic Republic, commonly known as East Germany. In addition, the Soviet Union conducted its own atomic bomb test in August 1949. The United States responded in 1952 with the first fusion nuclear bomb. The Soviets quickly answered with their own fusion nuclear test in 1953. The arms race of the Cold War was on.

North Atlantic Treaty Organization

Tensions mounted around the world as the Soviets consolidated their sphere of influence. In response, the West formed its own alliances, with the North Atlantic Treaty Organization (NATO) being the most extensive. NATO was formed in 1949 on the idea that an attack on any one member was considered to be an attack on all members. The original 12 members included Belgium, Canada, Denmark, France, Iceland, Italy, Luxembourg, Netherlands, Norway, Portugal, the United Kingdom, and the United States. Four other countries—Greece (1952), Turkey (1952), West Germany (1955), and Spain (1982)—joined NATO during the Cold War. Ten other countries joined NATO after the breakup of the Soviet Union. All 10 of these Eastern European countries were previously forced to be satellites of the Soviet Union.

Cold War Hot Wars

The standoff between the United States and the Soviet Union came to a head in many locations when wars took place. After World War II, the United States had a policy of containment. This meant that the United States tried to contain the Soviet threat. Two major early containment efforts were the Truman Doctrine and the Marshall Plan. The former was a promise to support Turkey and Greece militarily against Soviet threats. The Marshall Plan provided U.S. relief for rebuilding Europe. As the two superpowers vied for positioning around the world, the arms race continued and the space age was rapidly approaching. Fear of a nuclear war increased. But rather than fighting a giant war against one another, the two superpowers fought smaller regional wars. During the Cold War, both used the planet as a global chessboard for strategic moves.

Cold War battles took place in many locations. They were often fought through proxy nations that were the pawns in the half-century global struggle for dominance. While Germany had become a standoff between Soviet-supported East Germany and U.S.-supported West Germany, other fighting wars took place.

The Korean War was a very significant conflict. China, allied with the Soviet Union, supported the invasion of the southern part of the Korean Peninsula by the North in June 1950. With the Soviets boycotting the United Nations and Communist China not a member of the UN Security Council, the Security Council unanimously condemned the invasion of the South. The Soviet failure to use its veto meant that forces were convened to fight against the North with UN endorsement. A horrible three-year war followed. It ended leaving the Demilitarized Zone between North Korea and South Korea about the same as it had been before the war. However, it is estimated that the war cost 4 million casualties, including more than 50,000 U.S. soldiers.

Korea was not the last Cold War fight. Tensions increased further in 1956 when Soviet premier Nikita Khrushchev spoke to a gathering of ambassadors from the West. He boasted, "We will bury you!" Further, Khrushchev threatened the United States and its allies with nuclear war as he attempted to bully Western countries into submission. The Soviets invaded Hungary in 1956 to keep it in the Soviet orbit. However, the brief marriage between the Communist giants of China and the Soviet Union broke apart in 1956. This happened as Khrushchev and China's

MAKING CONNECTIONS

KEY PLAYERS IN THE UNITED STATES' RISE

The rise of the United States in the nineteenth and twentieth centuries was truly amazing. While most Americans contributed with their hard labor or in far-flung wars, some emerged as key leaders. Some led in government or by service, while others led in business and industry. Who do you believe were the three most important leaders during these two centuries? Defend your selections.

leader, Mao Tse-tung, both sought global leadership of the Communist movement. Later, in 1969, the two giants even fought border battles.

The Cold War had many features. The race to space and nuclear arms escalation were the most threatening. Blatant propaganda and monetary support were both used to influence neutral countries. Many of them were new nations just emerged from colonial status. Proxy wars were aided and often paid for by the two superpowers. Spy flights and bombers would test the defense systems of the adversary. The list is long. Many countries tired of the superpower squabbles and, in response, the Non-Aligned Movement (NAM) started in 1961. Member countries agreed not to align with superpowers. Today, the organization has nearly 120 members.

The Cuban Missile Crisis

Tensions between the United States and the Soviet Union reached the boiling point with the Cuban Missile Crisis in 1963. The Soviet Union had established an alliance with Fidel Castro in 1959 after the Cuban Revolution. A failed U.S. attempt to overthrow Castro's regime in 1961, called the Bay of Pigs Invasion, made Castro wary of his northern neighbor. Thus, he strengthened his ties to the Soviet Union. Khrushchev offered missiles to Cuba as protection and in response to U.S. missiles that had been placed in Turkey. In October 1962, the world stood on the brink of nuclear war when U.S. president John F. Kennedy ordered a naval blockade of Cuba. With the world fearing the worst, Khrushchev backed down and agreed to dismantle the missiles. However, unknown to the public, a secret deal had been negotiated between Kennedy and Khrushchev. This agreement was that the Soviets would withdraw the Cuban missiles if, in return, the United States promised not to invade Cuba and to withdraw its missiles from Turkey. The world breathed a sigh of relief. A possible nuclear nightmare had been avoided—but the Cold War would continue.

Vietnam War (1954–1975)

Another proxy superpower war was fought in Vietnam. Called the Vietnam War, or the Second Indochina War, it was another major Cold War conflict that lasted from 1954 to 1975. Here, the Soviets' chess piece was North Vietnam, while the United States supported South Vietnam. Using guerrilla warfare tactics and Soviet support, the north eventually prevailed in 1975 after the United States had removed its forces.

The Cold War was fought on fronts from Africa to Asia and Europe to the Americas. Both the United States and Soviet Union spent massive amounts of money in the arms and space races. However, while the two nations struggled for political supremacy,

MUTUAL ASSURED DESTRUCTION (MAD)

The United States rose in the twentieth century from a regional power to a global superpower. While much of this was due to the rapid economic and social development in the country, the military also made major advances. Today, the United States stands alone as the world's supreme military power.

While nuclear weapons greatly expanded the military strike force, these powerful weapons may have made themselves unusable. One result of the Cuban Missile Crisis was the recognition by the Soviet Union and the United States that both countries would be destroyed in a nuclear exchange. The notion of mutually assured destruction (MAD) means that the country striking first in a nuclear exchange would still be destroyed by the response of the other superpower. While MAD is not an adopted treaty, it provides a strong psychological reason for not using nuclear weapons and nuclear annihilation.

Examining the impact of defense missile systems may have an impact on MAD if a nation believes it can fend off the nuclear weapons fired by other countries. Follow this trend to find out whether antiballistic weapons fuel or threaten the idea of MAD.

something else was taking place. The capitalist economy of the United States was churning much more effectively than the Soviet Union's centrally run economy. Thus, the end of the Cold War came without a shot. How did this half-century conflict that once threatened the entire world end with a whimper?

THE FALL OF THE SOVIET UNION

The fall of the Soviet Union was world-shaking in terms of its impact. Long dominated by government management of all aspects of the economy, the country faced a financial crisis in the mid-1980s. Far-flung military ventures were expensive. Oil prices were low, bringing little revenue to the oil-rich Soviets. Worker productivity was low, and cooperative farms were poor producers. Thus, Soviet president Mikhail Gorbachev led the country to investigate new economic structures. Among these, he shifted money away from the military and toward the civilian economy. He allowed private ownership of property and businesses and pushed for greater openness. As a result, various parts of the Soviet Union became independent countries. A new Russia was born out of the debris of the Soviet Union, and the Cold War ended.

The fall of the Soviet Union led to the fall of the Berlin Wall in Germany. Germany reunited, and former parts of the Soviet Union became independent. These included new countries like Latvia, Lithuania, Estonia, Georgia, Ukraine, Belarus, Kazakhstan, Moldova, and others. Former Soviet satellites fell out of orbit and became truly independent. Thus, citizens of Hungary, Poland, Romania, Bulgaria, and others were able to create democratic societies that were not under Soviet control.

After the fall of the Soviet Union, the United States remained the last country standing as a superpower. With the world's largest economy and most dominant military, it stood unchallenged throughout the 1990s. How long would this situation last? How would the only superpower use its strength?

After decades of containing East German citizens, the Berlin Wall was torn down and Germany was reunited *(above)*. This symbolic act was part of the breakup of the Soviet Union, which left the United States as the most powerful country in the world.

THE WORLD'S POLICE?

One role ascribed to the United States after the Cold War was the world's police. Activities related to this role took place in the Persian Gulf when Iraq invaded the neighboring country of Kuwait in 1990. The United States quickly stepped in under the leadership of President George H.W. Bush. Iraqi forces were quickly dismantled and pushed back to near their capital city of Bagdad. Kuwait was restored, thanks to the U.S. action. Soon after achieving victory in the Gulf War, U.S. forces pulled out, rather than occupy the country. This police action was authorized by the United Nations, and the United States led the way in enforcing the will of the international organization.

The United States also engaged in a police action in the Balkans, where the former country of Yugoslavia exploded with nationalism and ethnic tensions in the early 1990s. The detestable practice called ethnic cleansing had Serbs, Croats, and Bosniaks torturing and killing each other in efforts to create individual states. President Bill Clinton ordered the United States to intervene and brokered the peace agreement that ended the fighting.

The United States has also intervened in other situations, with some being successful and others being severely criticized by the international community. As long as the United States is the world's only superpower, it will be criticized by many. They will ask, "Who made the United States the world's police?" Others, however, see the United States as the last best hope for democracies in the world. The United States' military and economic strength placed it in the position of global powerhouse as the twenty-first century dawned.

CHALLENGES OF THE TWENTY-FIRST CENTURY

The dawn of the twenty-first century was filled with promise for the United States, the world's only superpower. The country had the world's largest economy with a gross domestic product (GDP) standing at nearly $10 trillion. Its military was the world's strongest. The United States was respected overseas and still stood as a hopeful beacon beckoning immigrants from around the world. The crystal fortress image of the United States was soon to be shattered, however, by the actions of a terrorist organization called al Qaeda.

SEPTEMBER 11, 2001

It was a clear, beautiful morning in New York City on September 11, 2001. However, the day would soon turn deadly. In a matter of moments, al Qaeda conducted suicide air attacks on both towers of the World Trade Center. Terrorists hijacked two commercial airliners and flew them into the towering buildings. A third hijacked plane struck the Pentagon, the U.S. military headquarters. Passengers on a fourth plane overtook the hijacking al Qaeda terrorists and crashed the aircraft, keeping it from striking its target (thought to be the U.S. Capitol). With these unimaginable tragedies, life in the United States had changed forever.

The September 11 strikes were the worst on American lands since the Japanese attack on Pearl Harbor 60 years earlier. The idea of terrorists using commercial airplanes as bombs to fly into buildings was inconceivable before this date. While al Qaeda's strategy was diabolically brilliant, its heinous acts killed nearly 3,000 innocent people who were on board the planes or in the buildings.

What is the shadowy al Qaeda? It is a loose-knit radical Sunni Muslim organization started in 1988 and spearheaded by Osama bin Laden. Bin Laden directed the terrorist attack on the United States and, once again, a sleeping giant was awakened.

The people of the United States were horrified at the destruction and loss of human life caused by bin Laden and his al Qaeda organization. Nineteen men were responsible for the attacks, and ironically most had received their flight training in the United States. The nation came together as it had done after Pearl Harbor. Both Democrats and Republicans worked quickly to hold the perpetrators accountable. U.S. citizens joined together in a way that had not happened in recent decades. The United States was a nation united and clearly focused on improving national security and going after al Qaeda.

The Federal Bureau of Investigation (FBI), as well as the United Kingdom, quickly established that al Qaeda was responsible for the September 11 attacks. NATO came to the support of the United States as action was initiated in Afghanistan, where al Qaeda was hiding. Military operations quickly moved against al Qaeda and the Taliban government in Afghanistan, which harbored the terrorist organization. As this book is written, Osama bin Laden remains at large. He is believed to be hiding and directing operations from somewhere in the mountains between Afghanistan and Pakistan.

AFGHANISTAN AND PAKISTAN

In late 2001, President George W. Bush declared a War on Terror. This declaration had the objectives of countering and preventing terrorist attacks. It also aimed at limiting the influence and reach of terrorist organizations like al Qaeda. U.S. and NATO forces invaded Afghanistan late in 2001, forcing out the country's Taliban leaders. While the invading forces quickly dispatched the Taliban government, the Taliban and al Qaeda fled into the mountains of Pakistan, adjacent to Afghanistan. A democratic government was installed in Afghanistan.

The United States also engaged Pakistan and embraced its leader, Pervez Musharraf, as an ally in the War on Terror. It was a complicated situation. Military leader Musharraf had overthrown Pakistan's previous leader and appointed himself president. He was not elected, and indeed he suspended Pakistan's constitution. Yet, because he had agreed to take a stand against terrorism, many Western nations supported him. While Musharraf was a U.S. ally in the War on Terror, his people wanted a democratic government. On December 27, 2007, Benazir Bhutto, twice an elected prime minister of Pakistan, was assassinated by al Qaeda. Her assassination crushed the hopes of pro-democracy forces in Pakistan. It was also a setback for the United States, which saw her as a democratic hope for Pakistan in the fight against terrorism. Under threat of impeachment, Musharraf resigned as Pakistan's president in August 2008. Bhutto's husband, Asif Ali Zardari, was elected president in September 2008.

Many are critical of Pakistan because of the country's ineffective pursuit of al Qaeda and the Taliban in the mountains bordering Afghanistan. Thus, in 2008, the United States increased attacks inside Pakistan without approval from the Pakistanis. Both U.S. political parties agreed that more U.S. forces were

A Marine company in Afghanistan moves on after Operation Swift Freedom in November 2001. The United States was driven to declare war on Afghanistan's Taliban government and the terrorist group al Qaeda following the devastating attacks on September 11, 2001.

needed in Afghanistan. Therefore, fighting there will most likely continue into the second decade of the century.

IRAQ AND IRAN

The United States has long considered both Iraq and Iran to be sponsors of terrorism. Iraq had been suspect under the rule of Saddam Hussein since his invasion of Kuwait in 1990. He was believed to have weapons of mass destruction (WMD) since the Gulf War. However, proof was difficult to find. President George W. Bush pushed the United Nations to conduct WMD inspections in Iraq. Hussein stalled on these requests until 2002, when the Bush administration was pushing for an invasion of Iraq. In March 2003, the United States invaded Iraq without UN support. Hussein apparently had failed to abandon his WMD programs in nuclear arms and chemical weapons. However, in the end, the U.S. allegations were proven untrue.

The United States quickly won the war in Iraq, but had difficulty establishing peace in the country. Al Qaeda entered Iraq after the war started and again fought against the United States. The terrorist organization used suicide bombers to inflict heavy casualties on Americans and Iraqi civilians. An Iraqi rebellion against al Qaeda and a large U.S. troop surge in 2007 began to improve the situation in Iraq. However, the U.S. reputation in the international community was damaged; many people believed that the United States had invaded Iraq for reasons that proved to be untrue.

During the Iraqi conflict, Iran was aiding Iraq's Shiite Muslims. Roadside bombs and other weapons made in Iran were being provided to Iraq for use against the United States. At the same time, Iran was believed to be developing nuclear weapons. Iran claimed that its nuclear program was for electrical power, not bombs. Many fear that Iran could be the site of conflict in the future as the country pursues its nuclear dreams. U.S. interests in the region, including Israel, are strongly against an Iran armed with nuclear weapons and rockets that can deliver these devices. Thus, Iran remained suspect by the United States at the end of the first decade in the twenty-first century.

A NATION DIVIDED

While the United States had been very united after the attacks on September 11, the invasion of Iraq served to divide the country again. Many supported the war and the removal of Saddam Hussein. But some felt betrayed because WMDs were not found. These citizens felt they had been lied to in the rush to war with Iraq. Thus, as casualties and war costs mounted, many

Americans opposed the war and the Bush administration. Support for the troops remained strong, but many believed they were fighting in the wrong place. With bin Laden hiding somewhere in the mountains between Afghanistan and Pakistan, many Americans saw this area as being more important than Iraq.

When the 2004 presidential election took place, the nation reflected a sharp division between Republicans and Democrats. The election was similar to that of 2000, in which the candidate elected by the electoral college, George W. Bush, had fewer citizen votes than his opponent, Al Gore. While the country was very united after 9/11, much of the unity had been lost with the Iraq War. This division was also evident in the 2008 election.

THE MIDDLE EAST

The United States has had a long-standing interest in the welfare of Israel. Israel is a country surrounded by Islamic nations that are often hostile to it. Israel was carved out of Palestine by the United Nations in 1948. This action created a Jewish state (Israel) and an Arab state (Palestine). When Israel became independent, it was attacked by surrounding Arab nations. At the end of the war, Israel was larger, as it had taken nearly 80 percent of the Palestinian lands.

The United States continued to support Israel in other major Arab-Israeli wars in 1956, 1967, and 1973. This support has continued with border conflicts with Lebanon and the Palestinian Territories. Israel now has successful treaties with Egypt and Jordan, but extremist elements in Lebanon and the Gaza Strip continue to fight against Israeli interests. The United States has continued to promote peace in the region. But as a long-term ally of Israel, Arab nations do not believe the United States is a fair mediator. Thus, conflicts in the Middle East, the world's major source of oil, remain a U.S. concern.

The United States has also designated certain groups in the Middle East as terrorist organizations. Most prominent of these are the Islamic resistance group in Palestine, which is called Hamas, and Hizbollah ("party of God") in Lebanon. Both of these groups are based in countries bordering Israel, and both seek the destruction of Israel. Many of the members of Hamas were descendants of impoverished people who were displaced by Israel's war of independence. Numerous other terrorist

THE UNITED STATES AND ISLAM

The U.S. War on Terror has targeted terrorist Islamic organizations like al Qaeda. In addition, after the attacks on 9/11, many Americans became suspicious of Muslims in the United States. Living in a country claiming a predominantly Christian heritage, many Americans did not understand, and some even feared, Islam and Muslims. While the vast majority of Muslims practice their beliefs peacefully and with respect for others, some do not. This paradox has presented a challenge to the United States, which, according to the 2008 CIA *World Factbook*, is home to 0.6 percent of the world's Muslim population (about 1.8 million people). However, estimates of the U.S. Muslim population vary widely because the number is often used politically to promote fear or calm.

Americans will continue to face Islamic terrorists and domestic fears and questions. To participate intelligently in this discussion, U.S. citizens need to understand Islam and the problems posed by extremists. Talking with local Muslims and researching the religion can help Americans to understand the true threats and challenges posed by radical Islam as well as the understanding and compassion of moderate Islam. History shows that religious extremism has been practiced by many religious zealots, including Christians, Jews, Muslims, and others. Fortunately, these extremists do not represent the true nature of these faiths, but, in the hands of radicals, their faith has been abducted for violent purposes. Understanding and opposing these twenty-first-century threats is also vital to the security of Americans and the world.

organizations also operate in the Middle East with the intent of destroying Israel. As a strong ally of Israel, the United States has labeled many of these groups terrorist organizations.

NORTH KOREA

North Korea has been a thorn in the side of the United States since the Korean conflict. Since the end of the war, there have been tens of thousands of violations of the Demilitarized Zone

Kim Jong Il is seen thumbing his nose in this political cartoon. On his fingers are detonating nuclear weapons. The cartoon indicates that the North Korean leader has little regard for the United States and other countries attempting to put a halt to his nuclear program.

(DMZ) that separates North and South Korea. The DMZ is a 2.5-mile-wide (4 km) unoccupied strip established after the war to divide the North and South. Today, the DMZ is still the most militarized border in the world.

Today, the threat posed by North Korea extends to nuclear arms. In October 2006, North Korea tested a nuclear device in the northeastern part of the country. The United Nations, the United States, and other countries pressured North Korea into negotiations with the intent of having the nuclear program dismantled. Efforts to dismantle North Korea's nuclear program were initiated in 2008. However, numerous North Korean roadblocks have continued to hamper the program's elimination. The United States remains a strong ally of South Korea. Therefore, the United States maintains a military presence in the South and views hostile efforts by North Korea with great suspicion.

THE RISE OF CHINA

Another rising challenge to the United States in the twenty-first century is China, the world's most populated country. With 1.3 billion people and a rapidly expanding economic base, China had the world's fourth-largest economy by 2007. Soon, its economy will pass that of Germany and Japan. It will then trail only the United States in terms of annual GDP. In 2008, China's annual economic growth rate was an astounding 11 percent. Many experts believe that China will soon overtake the United States as the world's largest economy.

China also holds a large amount of the United States' national debt—more than $500 million in 2008. (This issue will be explored further in Chapter 6.) Only Japan held more U.S. Treasury securities. This means that China and other nations can affect the value of the U.S. dollar and have added influence over U.S. monetary policies.

A rising China means that another superpower is looming on the horizon. With economic prosperity, military power often follows. China has been rapidly modernizing its military and is testing U.S. readiness. From strikes by Chinese computer hackers on U.S. computer networks to antisatellite tests, China's increasing capabilities threaten U.S. interests. China's continued military advances could present important challenges for U.S. foreign and economic policy.

RUSSIA ON THE RISE

The Soviet Union disintegrated in 1991. At the time, it seemed like a crippling blow to the new Russian state. However, with surging prices of oil and natural gas in the twenty-first century, resource-rich Russia restarted its economic engine. Under the

MAKING CONNECTIONS

THE WAR ON TERROR

September 11, 2001, changed the United States forever. The attack changed the way that the country conducts activities inside and outside its borders. Use the Internet to investigate the following questions about how the United States has conducted the War on Terror that was declared by President George W. Bush in 2001.

- What are the U.S. objectives in the War on Terror?
- Who are U.S. allies in the War on Terror?
- Who is the war being conducted against and where?
- What have been the successes and failures of the War on Terror in:
  - The United States
  - The Middle East
  - Asia and the Pacific
  - Europe
  - Africa

leadership of Vladimir Putin, Russia rose from the ashes of an unworkable Communist economic system. Russia's economic rise also fueled new efforts to modernize its military.

The resurrection of Russia became starkly evident in August 2008 when Russian forces went to war with Georgia, a small neighboring country. The Russians attempted to defend their aggressive military actions. They said that ethnic cleansing had been taking place in the Georgian provinces of South Ossetia and Abkhazia. Most of the people in these regions favor inclusion in the Russian Federation but were citizens of Georgia.

The Russian military's actions sent a chilling message to other bordering countries. Lands such as Poland, Hungary, Romania, and others once again felt the heavy and threatening hand of Russia. Many of these former Soviet satellite countries have sought membership in NATO. Were Russia to attack any of them, the United States could be drawn directly into the fray. Thus, the resurgence of Russia poses another major security issue for the United States and its allies in the twenty-first century.

AMERICA'S RESOURCES AND RICHES

The United States' resource bounty is one of the major reasons the country has established itself as a world power. What are resources? They include both human and natural elements. Human resources are the people living in a country. In the United States, citizens serve as a rich pool of people who are educated, creative, and hardworking. They possess the work ethic and entrepreneurial spirit necessary for a great nation. Citizens provide the labor, management, ingenuity, and capital essential to development. They also provide many other important human traits necessary to make use of their environment, including the country's natural resources.

Natural resources include a wide variety of elements that are available in a country's natural environment. These natural elements can be as diverse as air, wind, water, climate, soil, vegetation, minerals, fish, and wildlife. These elements become natural resources when people use them. Sunshine was just sunshine until humans started to use the rays of the sun to generate energy. Thus, sunshine is now a natural resource for many people. The same is true of wind, water, tides, coal, gold, and an array of other elements that are used today by people as natural resources.

The United States occupies the world's third-largest land area with 3,794,083 square miles (9,826,630 sq km). The land stretches from the North Slope of Alaska to the tip of the Florida Peninsula and from the sun-swept beaches of Hawaii to the craggy coast of Maine. This vast area holds a cornucopia of natural and human resources that have helped the United States become a great nation. This chapter explores some of the resources that have helped to put the country on the path to greatness.

NATURAL RESOURCES

The United States has been blessed with an environment rich in natural resources. Although all are not available in the amounts that are needed, the country still has a vast supply of important resources that Americans have tapped to improve their lives and their country. Primary among these are the country's abundant land, water, and air.

The Land

European colonists quickly took advantage of the rich soils and established a farming tradition in the young nation. As the country stretched westward, new lands were added, including the United States' midwestern "breadbasket." Today, the country's farmlands and ranches feed not only the United States, but also much of the world. The United States is the world's leading agricultural power. This has happened even as the number of farmers has dropped below 1 percent of the population. In addition to farming and ranching, Americans now use their lands for recreation, transportation, commercial ventures, and public space.

The rich soils, adequate water supplies, and varied climates have allowed the United States to farm a wide variety of products.

U.S. ranking in grain production includes corn (#1), wheat (#3), oats (#3), and rye and barley (#6). The United States is the world's leading producer of soybeans. Vegetables include onions, beans, peas, carrots, beets, lettuce, chilies, cabbage, potatoes, and many others. The country is a leading producer of many fruits, including strawberries and prunes (made from plums) (#1); oranges, apples, cherries, and grapefruit (#2); and pears, peaches, and nectarines (#3). Thus, the rich lands and work of farmers produces bountiful crops that feed the country and many others around the world.

The lands also serve to provide ranch lands, forests, and other environments that support both wildlife and farm animals. Hunting and fishing remain popular sports for many, with rich environments for wildlife. Farmers raise cattle, sheep, swine, chickens, turkeys, and many other specialty animals for the market. Even ostrich, llama, and buffalo are raised commercially.

There also are lands that provide a wealth of minerals that are used for energy and industry. Coal, uranium, petroleum, and natural gas are plentiful and supply much of the nation's energy. Important nonfuel mineral resources include rich deposits of copper, iron, silver, gold, potash, phosphates, and others. Forests also provide timber for paper and lumber. Thus, the dazzling array of resources provided by the lands in the United States has contributed greatly to the country's economic strength.

Water

Freshwater is vital for life. It nurtures crops and animal life. Water also can provide energy, recreation, food sources, and transportation. The United States has a number of freshwater sources that are natural and many others made by humans. For example, hydroelectric dams hold needed water and can generate energy that does not pollute the atmosphere. According to the U.S. Army Corps of Engineers, there are 79,000 dams in the country. These dams often distribute freshwater to surrounding farmlands and urban areas.

The Black Thunder Coal Mine in Wyoming *(above)* is one of the world's largest. The United States is a vast land that boasts a great supply of natural resources.

Virtual underground lakes, called aquifers, have also supplied cities and farms with needed water. The Ogallala Aquifer in the central United States is one of the world's largest, but it is rapidly being depleted due to excess use. However, a number of aquifers in the country still supply a lifeline of freshwater to farms and municipalities.

Freshwater lakes are another source in many areas of the United States. These include the sizable Great Lakes, located between the United States and Canada, as well as thousands of smaller lakes that dot the landscape. These lakes and the surrounding areas are also great recreation areas, with fishing, boating, skiing, and other activities. Many also provide water to local farms and communities.

Great rivers are another resource in the United States. From the waters of the Mississippi and the Missouri to thousands of small creeks, these flowing streams provide life to humans, plants, and animals. Larger rivers provide transportation means to the sea and between communities. Thousands of communities depend upon these rivers for water and sewage disposal. In the west, thousands of acres of farmland depend upon rivers as the source of irrigation water. Fishing and recreation also prevail on many rivers, as they provide for many types of human usage.

Freshwater is not the only asset that the United States has. The Pacific, Atlantic, and Arctic oceans border the United States and provide other benefits. Some of these are related to important transportation systems by use of the sea. Others relate to the seafood that helps feed the American people. Underneath many of these seas are valuable resources like oil and natural gas.

MAKING CONNECTIONS

IDENTIFYING LOCAL RESOURCES AND NEEDS

Local examples are useful in understanding the impact of human and natural resources. Research the following questions to examine the resources and needs in your local and state regions.

- ➔ What natural resources are found in your community and surrounding area? Where do these resources go?
- ➔ What are the key natural resources produced or found in your state? What resources are exported?
- ➔ What types of work do people in your community do? What careers do young people aspire to?
- ➔ What educational opportunities exist in your community or region that help to develop human resources?
- ➔ What are the jobs being done by new Americans? Are immigrants significant in your community in meeting human resource needs? Why or why not?

The United States has 12,380 miles (19,924 km) of valuable coastline. This coastline has many important ports and harbors, along with many recreational opportunities. Seattle, San Francisco, and San Diego are important natural harbors on the Pacific Coast. Boston, New York, and Philadelphia occupy protected havens on the Atlantic. Seaports serve the country as key sites for import and export trade.

The Air

Even the atmosphere is a valuable asset. Earth's varied climates create environments for growing many different crops. Airplanes fly across the country's vast airspace. Today, satellites roam the skies providing television, telephone, and radio signals to homes and businesses. These are just some of the ways in which the sky is important.

Clean air also helps to provide a good place for American citizens to live. While pollution has increased in recent decades, the United States still has air that is better than much of the world.

HUMAN RESOURCES

The United States' most important resource is its people. They are what have made the country great. Americans have used their environment to construct communication and transportation systems that link the people of the country. Transportation connections come in the air with airlines, on the land with rail and roads, and on the water with various watercraft. Communication systems go under the water, on and under the land, and through the air with telecommunications, television, and radio. Huge networks have advanced the connections between places and people in the United States. This human-created infrastructure has created agricultural, industrial, and service jobs that employ the United States' talented labor pool.

History has shown that Americans are hard workers. From early colonists to the present day, people have worked hard to succeed and prevail, often against difficult odds. U.S. ingenuity has put men on the moon and connected people around the world though the World Wide Web. Great American inventors include Benjamin Franklin, Thomas Edison, Samuel Morse, Henry Ford, and Alexander Graham Bell. Others include Cyrus McCormick, Robert Goddard, the Wright brothers, Eli Whitney, Jonas Salk, and Steve Wozniak. Even the sport of basketball was created by a Canadian—James Naismith—who became an American citizen. U.S. ingenuity has served the country well in war and peace, and in prosperity and poverty. This creative talent has carried into all fields. The United States is a world leader in science, business, government, the arts, and social sciences.

What is the résumé of the U.S. population? The country has a high literacy rate, at 99 percent, and Americans can expect to have an average of 16 years of school—one of the highest levels in the world. In contrast to many countries where the education of women is limited, U.S. women actually average more education than their male counterparts. U.S. education is universal at the elementary and secondary level, and the quality of U.S. universities is the envy of the world.

As a land of opportunity, the country has also been blessed with immigrants from around the world. This cultural diversity provides a variety of backgrounds and experiences that make the United States stronger. In addition, many of these immigrants maintain overseas contacts, which are used for business ventures. While the dreams of women and minorities are limited in many societies, the United States has been a beacon of opportunity. Thus, in many communities across the United States, you will find new and talented Americans. Whether they be a Hispanic lawyer, an Indian engineer, an Egyptian cab driver, a Filipino nurse, or a Chinese doctor, all are now Americans contributing to make the United States great.

POLITICAL LEGACIES

As a democracy with a constitution that has prevailed for more than 220 years, the United States has had remarkable political stability. Why is this important? A stable democracy usually brings openness in government institutions. This quality is called transparency, and it promotes honesty in government. An additional factor is the rule of law, which puts all individuals under the law. Even elected U.S. leaders are held accountable for breaking the law.

The U.S. political system allows for checks and balances between the branches of government. The Constitution provides for the legislative, judicial, and executive branches to look over

The U.S. political system allows for a stable government, which in turn results in a stable society. Above, the U.S. Congress meets at the Capitol in 2008.

each other's actions and counterbalance excesses. This has happened frequently in U.S. history. It promotes political stability and prevents individuals or institutions from overreaching their constitutional powers.

Political stability and trust in the U.S. dollar encourages other countries to invest in U.S. businesses and government debt. Even in the economic turmoil that began in 2008, the U.S. government stepped in to calm stock markets and assure investors worldwide. When U.S. markets stumble, their action

OIL AND THE UNITED STATES

The United States is a huge importer of oil. What hope exists for more oil development in the country? Actually, there are many opportunities for developing the country's oil deposits. But the costs of bringing them to the market are higher than the oil that was easily found and produced in the past. Some believe that the environmental trade-offs of producing these new sources are too high. Many Americans also believe that the United States should be investing in new technologies and energy sources. Where are the country's new oil possibilities?

- **Outer Continental Shelf.** One area of great potential lies off the U.S. coast on the Outer Continental Shelf areas controlled by the federal government. The Minerals Management Service (MMS), a division of the U.S. Department of the Interior, estimates that the country has between 67 and 115 billion barrels of oil offshore. However, some of this oil may be too expensive to extract. Many Americans also fear environmental damage if hurricanes, human error, or other disasters strike and pollute the oceans and Gulf of Mexico.
- **Arctic National Wildlife Refuge.** Great attention has been given to the oil located in northern Alaska's Arctic National Wildlife Refuge (ANWR). While an important site for oil, the Energy Information Administration estimated in 2008 that

echoes through stock markets worldwide. The U.S. political system has repeatedly been an anchor to stabilize these markets.

RESOURCE CHALLENGES

While the United States has benefited from its many natural and human resources, some resources are in short supply. Oil is an obvious example, because much today is imported from Canada,

the area contains only about 4.3 billion barrels of oil. This represents only a small fraction of the amount that could be produced on the Outer Continental Shelf. While drilling in the rugged Arctic environment has been difficult, oil companies have successfully addressed the environmental issues they have faced. However, questions linger about the environmental impact of drilling in the ANWR, and these cause oil production in the area to be held up in the U.S. Congress.

➲ **Oil shale reserves.** The greatest U.S. oil reserves are held in the Green River Formation's oil shale in Colorado, Wyoming, and Utah. Other oil shale deposits also exist elsewhere. The amount of oil is huge when compared to the earlier mentioned potential sources. The Rand Corporation estimated in 2008 that the Green River Formation alone holds between 500 billion and 1.1 *trillion* barrels of oil. Two major challenges exist for extracting this oil. First, it is much more expensive to extract oil from shale than from other types of wells. Second, the environmental impact is much greater than oil obtained by other means. With the world's largest shale oil reserves, the United States is sitting on a virtual ocean of oil. Many question whether the financial and environmental costs will be too high to actually use it.

Mexico, Nigeria, Saudi Arabia, Venezuela, and Iraq. Only three decades ago, the United States supplied more than 70 percent of its own oil. By 2008, more than 60 percent was imported. This represents a tremendous outflow of U.S. dollars, with much of it going to regimes that are hostile to the United States. Many in the United States wonder why more is not being done to utilize the country's own immense shale deposits and tar sands to produce oil. Others promote more offshore drilling in U.S. waters. Still others claim that a new economy should be built on new energies like solar, wind, and wave power. In any case, the present economy is very reliant upon oil, a resource that has become much more expensive in recent years.

Another emerging resource challenge is in professional and technical fields needed in the United States. The September 11, 2001, attacks on the United States have made immigration and travel to the country more difficult for foreigners. Thus, the country has not been able to produce enough engineers, doctors, and nurses, among others, to meet current demand. The inadequacy of human resources can limit science and the construction of necessary infrastructure to keep the United States advancing in the global marketplace.

As the United States advances into the twenty-first century, the global competition for natural and human resources will become more intense. The country still has many valuable resources. They can be used to advance the country and its agendas in the coming century. But many new challenges are emerging. These challenges may require the role of the United States to change to meet the needs of the country and its people.

AMERICA'S GLOBAL ECONOMIC ROLE

The United States has stamped its economic imprint on the world. At first glimpse, a traveler overseas will see U.S. business ventures like McDonald's, Burger King, KFC, Pizza Hut, Coca-Cola, Pepsi-Cola, and many others. The U.S. impact, however, reaches far beyond these obvious U.S. business interests.

The United States possesses the world's largest economy, with a gross domestic product (GDP) that approached $14 *trillion* in 2008. How much is this? If you stretched one-dollar bills end to end, you would have a string of dollars that would stretch to the sun and back—seven times! Since the United States is a world leading economic power, the impact of the country's gigantic economy on the world is staggering.

In this chapter we will examine the United States' economic role in today's world. We will also investigate how this role and its impact are changing. If you haven't guessed, this chapter will talk a lot about money. It will focus upon ways that U.S. wealth has been utilized around the world. Let us begin our trillions of dollars' journey.

THE WORLD'S ENTREPRENEUR

The United States has a free market economy that primarily practices capitalism. Capitalism is an economic system in which property is owned privately and profit is a motive for business ventures. A free market allows buyers and sellers to agree on a price in the marketplace. For example, when you go shopping, the merchant offers a number of good and products. A set price is usually posted. However, a second store down the street may offer a lower price. Buying on the Internet may bring an even lower price. When you decide to buy the product from a particular seller, the transaction is completed, as you have agreed to pay their price. Negotiations may also take place with a merchant as the buyer tries to get a lower price or special features provided in addition to the merchant's original price.

The global economy operates as a huge marketplace with millions of transactions taking place every day. Goods and services are bought and sold as buyers and sellers agree on prices and complete their transactions. With the huge size of the United States' economy, U.S. businesses play a major role in the world's economic marketplace.

An entrepreneur is a person who starts or finances new business ventures. He or she assumes financial risk because the venture may be successful or may fail miserably. With a relatively free market, U.S. businesses have been able to take risks that would be more risky in many areas of the world. In the United States, entrepreneurs have been able to provide or obtain the financing needed to start up new businesses. Many of these ideas have taken root and have spread around the world. As examples, think of Microsoft, Google, International Business Machines (IBM), Yahoo!, Boeing, YouTube, eBay, McDonald's, Dell, and thousands of others. The creativity of the

FAST-FOOD WORLD

The United States has brought fast food to the world. The widening swath covered by U.S. fast-food companies like McDonald's, Burger King, Wendy's, KFC, Pizza Hut, Starbucks, and others is staggering in size and still growing.

McDonald's alone has more than 31,000 restaurants in more than 100 countries. These include stores on every continent (except Antarctica). Expansion is particularly rapid in China, where the taste for fast food is exploding. In fact, the world's largest McDonald's restaurant is located in Beijing, China. Worldwide, more than 47 million people are served each day by the company.

McDonald's offers amazing consistency in terms of quality but often adapts its menu to local tastes. Thus, vegetarian burgers are available at McDonald's in India. In Germany (and many other countries), one can get a beer or glass of wine with a burger. You can get a Maharaja burger in India, a rice burger in Hong Kong (the burger is placed in between rice cakes instead of a bun), and a pita-like creation called a Greek Mac in Greece. This global fast-food empire started with a single store just a half century ago.

Other fast-food companies have also rippled across the world. KFC was started in 1952 by Colonel Harland Sanders. Today, there are more than 11,000 KFCs in more than 80 countries, and a new KFC opens in China every other day. Pizza Hut is the world's largest pizza chain, with more than 34,000 restaurants in more than 100 countries. It began with a single pizzeria in 1958. Burger King, the world's second-largest burger chain, has more than 11,000 stores in nearly 70 countries. In Australia, the 300-plus Burger King franchises are called Hungry Jack, as the Burger King name was taken earlier by another company. Starbucks is a recent entry to the world marketplace of U.S. fast-food chains. Started in 1971 in Seattle, Washington, the chain now has more than 15,000 stores in more than 40 countries. Other fast-food companies, like Taco Bell, Long John Silver's, Subway, and Wendy's, are also international companies.

United States' successful entrepreneurs has been spread around the world and impacts the daily life of nearly all people on the planet.

THE U.S. DOLLAR: A GLOBAL CURRENCY

For decades, the primary world currency has been the U.S. dollar. Whether in a remote African village or a sprawling Asian city, the dollar reigned supreme as a world currency for much of the twentieth century. Many factors have contributed to this role. These include political stability in the United States, historical strength of the dollar, and a low inflation rate. All of these factors made the dollar the world's most trusted currency and one that would preserve its value. Thus, important world commodities such as petroleum traditionally have been priced in U.S. dollars.

During the last decades of the twentieth century, other currencies started to strengthen against the U.S. dollar. These included the German mark, the British pound, and the Japanese yen. While the U.S. dollar entered the new century as the world's currency, cracks soon began to appear in the international use of the currency. Why has this happened?

A number of reasons have contributed to the decreasing trust in the dollar, but four factors stand out. First, there has been a sharp rise in the strength of the new currency of the European Union (EU). Called the euro, this new currency made its debut in 1999 as an accounting device. On January 1, 2002, euro coins and currency started being used in the EU. The economy of the combined countries in the EU is comparable to that of the United States. Therefore, the euro has gained widespread acceptance as a stable currency.

Second is the U.S. government's ballooning fiscal deficit (discussed later in more detail). This governmental borrowing has made the dollar easier to obtain and has caused its value to fall against the euro and other currencies.

German officials press the "start" button to symbolize the transition from the deutsche mark to the euro as Germany's official currency in 1999. The U.S. dollar is the world's main currency, but the euro has risen quickly to second place.

A third factor is the amount the United States is spending on wars in Iraq and Afghanistan. In addition to costing hundreds of billions of dollars, the world's distrust of the United States (hence, its currency) increased as many overseas viewed the U.S. invasion of Iraq unfavorably.

A fourth factor is the financial institution crisis that hit the United States, and later the world, in 2008. All of these elements and others created questions about the stability and value of the U.S. dollar.

As a result of the stress on the U.S. dollar, the currency dropped in value against many other world currencies like the euro. In January 2002, a single euro could be bought for US$0.85—less than one dollar. In contrast, in April 2008, one euro cost U.S.$1.59. Thus, after only six years, one euro cost nearly twice as much in U.S. dollars. The U.S. dollar fell dramatically against most world currencies in the first decade of the twenty-first century. This means that imports cost more, but exports from the United States were also increased. For the dollar, though, it means that foreigners holding dollars can buy a lot more from the United States, including land, ports, airports, and businesses. Thus, U.S. assets can be bought cheaper by foreigners because of the declining value of the dollar. In addition, other countries are less likely to hold U.S. dollars because of their decreasing value. Even pricing oil in dollars is questioned by oil-producing countries awash in dollars they already hold.

Still, for now, the U.S. dollar is the world's main currency. The new contender, the euro, has made amazing advances and is now placed as the world's second-most held currency. Euros are increasingly valued around the world as a stable and trusted currency. If the dollar's fall from favor continues, this, too, could negatively affect the country's economy.

BUSINESS EXPORTS TO THE WORLD

While the United States is still a major producer of goods and services, its role has changed in recent decades. The change has been somewhat dramatic, as labor, one of the four fundamental factors of production (the others are land, capital, and entrepreneurship), has been increasingly outsourced. This means that jobs are being shipped overseas. This happens because, in today's global economy, labor is often cheaper overseas than in the United States. Accessibility has increased because of improved transportation and the Internet, which allows for telecommuting around the world. Thus, a writer in Malaysia can write books for an Australian publisher and exchange manuscripts instantaneously. Or a physician in India can record the notes of a U.S. doctor who is sleeping halfway around the world. With labor costs cheaper overseas, everything from cars to T-shirts can be produced more cheaply outside of the United States. However, this situation may be changing, and this trend will be explored later.

However, the United States is still a major exporter. These exports represent a variety of items, including agricultural products such as grains, fruits, tobacco products, and meat. The country is a leading exporter of airplanes and automobiles. It is also a leader in computers, music, movies, medicine, telecommunications equipment, and many other products. The United States also exports expertise, as many U.S. companies and individuals have the technical knowledge to help in activities ranging from deep-water oil drilling to cosmetics. Companies like Procter and Gamble, Boeing, Microsoft, Yahoo!, Google, Coca-Cola, Ford, General Electric, and thousands of others serve as exporters of goods or services.

Capital goods like computers, vehicle parts, aircraft, and telecommunications equipment make up nearly half of U.S. exports. Consumer goods represent about 15 percent of the total, while industrial supplies account for more than one-fourth of the total exports. Agriculture represents only about 9 percent of the country's exports.

Where do U.S. exports go? The most important importers are neighbors Canada and Mexico. Canada is the main recipient, with more than 22 percent of U.S. exports. Mexico follows with nearly 13 percent. Other export partners, in rank order, are

Japan, China, and the United Kingdom. The Netherlands, Germany, Belgium, France, and Singapore round out the country's top-ten export partners.

IMPORTS FROM THE WORLD

Imports are the goods and services that are brought into the United States. Such items increased greatly during the last

MAKING C●NNECTI●NS

YOUR COMMUNITY AND THE WORLD

The United States is today enmeshed in countless activities around the world. Much of this activity is economic, while other activities may be cultural, political, or social. In any case, your community is linked with the world in a wide variety of ways.

This chapter has examined some of the economic connections that the United States has with the world. Make a list of economic activities that connect your community to the world. The following questions will help to guide you:

- List countries that provide products available in your community.
- Identify the countries that local companies conduct business with.
- In a search for work, from what countries have immigrants come to your community?
- Do local transportation systems connect with other places in the world? Where?
- What other economic connections did you find between your community and the world?

decades of the twentieth century. In fact, their dollar value greatly exceeded that of U.S. exports. This left the United States with a huge trade deficit that ballooned to over $800 billion in 2007.

What does the United States import? The main categories are industrial supplies (33 percent), consumer goods (32 percent), capital goods (30 percent), and agricultural products (5 percent). Crude oil is considered an industrial supply. Since the United States is the world's largest consumer of oil, millions of dollars are being sent overseas to pay for the increasing costs of gasoline and other petroleum products. With only 5 percent of the world's population, the U.S. consumes nearly 25 percent of the world's oil. China is a very distant second. Thus, the effect of rising oil and gas prices sends more U.S. dollars out of the country to places like Canada, Saudi Arabia, Mexico, Venezuela, Nigeria, and other countries. Canada is the largest U.S. supplier of oil.

Many other imports are easily found in your home and may include computers and related products, clothing, cars, televisions, foods, and toys. Even souvenirs bought at U.S. tourist sites are made overseas—often in China. All of these imports contribute to the U.S. trade deficit. The list of main U.S. trading partners for imports is similar to the export list of countries. Canada and China are the two leading sources of imports with about 16 percent each in 2006. Mexico, Japan, and Germany are the next leading import partners.

THE BULGING NATIONAL DEBT

The U.S. government has the largest financial debt in all of history. This fact weighs not only on the United States and its citizens, but also on the minds of other countries. Much of this debt is owed to U.S. citizens who own government bonds. However, a huge amount is held by other countries.

What is debt, and how has it gotten so high for the United States? Basically, debt grows when a country or individual spends more than it takes in. For an individual, it would be like using credit cards and not paying off the balance each month. Interest is added, and the debt grows if more and more purchases are made. The same is true of the United States. The government has borrowed increasing amounts of money, but it has not taken in enough in taxes to balance the budget. Thus, the shortage is borrowed from individuals and countries in the form of bonds, which pay interest to the investors. According to the U.S. Treasury Department, by December 16, 2008, the national debt was a whopping $10,597,068,737,927.10. This means that there is a staggering debt of $34,447 for every man, woman, and child in the country—and it increases every day! To find out the national debt today, check the U.S. Treasury site "Debt to the Penny" at http://www.treasurydirect. gov/NP/BPDLogin?application=np.

Most of the outlandish deficit growth has taken place since 1980, when the debt stood at $930 billion dollars. By 1990, it had grown to $3,233 trillion, because President Reagan cut taxes, resulting in the deficit greatly increasing. The debt increased $1.5 trillion during President Clinton's time in office. But he left office with a budget surplus of $230 billion, the largest ever. With tax cuts, the attack on September 11, 2001, and the invasion of Iraq, President George W. Bush's budgets quickly took the nation into deficit spending. This and the financial crisis doubled the national debt during his presidency.

Much of the debt is owed to U.S. citizens who own treasury bills, U.S. savings bonds, and other bonds and instruments. Foreign governments also hold large amounts of these bonds and borrowing devices. Japan, China, Brazil, Russia, the United Kingdom, OPEC (Organization of Petroleum Exporting Countries) nations, and a wide array of other governments and their citizens own U.S. government securities. Thus, the U.S. deficit is financed by many of the friends of the country, but also by some who are hostile to the United States.

The impact of the huge U.S. national debt also contributes to inflation. Borrowing has made more dollars available. But too many dollars chasing goods and services means that businesses raise prices when dollars are less scarce than other currencies. Money is like other goods in that it operates according to supply and demand. If governments run their printing presses to make more money, the money eventually becomes less valuable. Thus, it takes more dollars to buy a barrel of oil, a new television, or video games. The debt also means that the country has fewer funds available to provide services, like health care or improving the military, to the American people. Fewer dollars are available each day. As *USA Today* reported in 2007, the U.S. deficit grows by over a million dollars a minute. The long-term effect of this debt may be very damaging to the health of the U.S. government, the dollar, and the economy.

CURRENT PROBLEMS AND PATTERNS

The United States belongs to a number of trade organizations and has signed many trade agreements. Many of these agreements take down trade barriers between countries. For example, many times in the past, the United States has put a tariff on goods coming into the country. A tariff is a duty or tax levied on imported or exported goods. The higher the tariff, the less likely that trade will take place, since the price of the goods is raised to include the tariff costs. Recent decades have seen a decrease in trade barriers, but some believe that this has also caused other problems.

One of these problems is U.S. manufacturing jobs being out-sourced, or going overseas. Tariffs have often been used to raise the price of foreign goods so that U.S. manufacturers can stay competitive. Other countries do this, too. For example, Japan taxes selected imported food products so that cheaper imports do not cause Japanese farmers to go out of business. Thus, some

This photograph of the national debt clock in New York City's Times Square was taken in 2002. The clock was retired around 2000, when the U.S. economy faced a surplus, but was reinstated when the debt began to grow again. Currently, the national debt is so large that there is not room to display it on the clock.

believe that the reduction or elimination of tariffs by the United States in the North American Free Trade Agreement (NAFTA) and other trade agreements has taken away U.S. jobs and moved them overseas.

Many factories have also left the United States to pursue cheaper labor costs in places like China, India, Malaysia, the Philippines, and Singapore. Some corporations have also moved their offices out of the United States to avoid paying U.S. taxes.

In addition, there are still many illegal economic activities taking place around the world. The U.S. dollar is often the currency used for these transactions. The U.S. government works with banks around the world to curtail these activities. For example, illegal drugs continue to plague the United States. Billions of dollars of drug-related activity takes place beyond the country's borders.

Another issue of importance has been illegal immigration into the United States from Mexico. Most of these illegal immigrants are merely seeking work to provide for their families. U.S. employers unlawfully hire these workers because the labor is cheap. However, after September 11, 2001, the country became increasingly concerned about illegal entries. The concern is that terrorists could enter the country in similar ways. Thus, a variety of efforts have taken place to address this issue.

Another area of concern is the sale of U.S. assets and businesses to foreign corporations. The dropping value of the dollar made purchasing U.S. companies much cheaper. Thus, foreign interests bought utilities, real estate, and even Budweiser, the United States' largest brewing company, in the first decade of the twenty-first century. Middle Eastern governments raised national security concerns when they attempted to buy U.S. ports and airports. These takeovers are further consequences of the rising U.S. debt and falling dollar.

Even with all of the changes in the U.S. economy, the country's role in the world's economy is still immense. Stock market vibrations that begin in the United States echo across the world

in seconds. Problems of the dollar in the early twenty-first century careened around the world, affecting oil, food, housing,
and other markets. Economic transactions involving the country
number in the millions each day. They range from simple money
transfers to international trade and illegal activities like traffick-
ing in drugs and weapons. In terms of economics, the United
States is like a rock that is thrown into a lake. First there is the
splash, and then there are the ripples. Thus, the role of the United
States in economic terms is like the rock as it sends waves of
economic activity across the planet.

AMERICA'S POLITICAL ROLE IN THE WORLD

The evolving role of the United States in today's world has become increasingly complex. Many of these arrangements are complicated by hostile adversaries. Both public and private bodies are involved in U.S. foreign relations. As you have seen, each day thousands of businesses work and trade with others around the world. At the same time, the master facilitator of U.S. foreign relations is the U.S. government.

Many parts of the federal government have responsibilities that link them to the rest of the world. From the spy agencies like the Central Intelligence Agency (CIA) to the U.S. Department of Agriculture (USDA), the international work of the government runs from the exotic to the mundane. This chapter presents a few of these political relationships and explores U.S. foreign policy in the twenty-first century.

U.S. FOREIGN POLICY

Previous chapters have shown how U.S. foreign policy has evolved from its early isolationist tendencies to become very engaged globally. The primary agency of the government charged with the day-to-day operation of foreign relations is the U.S. Department of State. The State Department is under the executive branch of government. It is headed by the secretary of state, who serves on the president's cabinet. In addition to implementing U.S. foreign policy, the State Department is also responsible for passports, travel warnings, youth exchange programs, embassies, and consulates.

The policies of the United States are constantly adjusting to meet the needs of the country and its allies. These policies reach around the world and include some of the following key features:

- The War on Terror and prevention of attacks on the United States and its allies
- Advocacy for democracy and human rights
- Positions on regional conflicts like those in Israel and Iraq
- Prevention of the spread of weapons of mass destruction (WMD)
- Expansion of free trade and free markets
- Development of a national security system that addresses the needs of the twenty-first century
- Strategic foreign policy positions for the continents and countries

To research these positions and others, consult the U.S. Department of State Web site.

U.S. MILITARY

The military is a vital tool for promoting U.S. political interests overseas and at home. The Department of Defense (DoD) is the

U.S. secretary of state Hillary Clinton meets with Chinese premiere Wen Jiabao in Beijing in 2009. The U.S. state department implements U.S. foreign policy; the secretary of state is crucial to helping America maintain its role in the world.

executive branch agency with oversight over the United States' military machine. The department is headed by the secretary of defense. According to the U.S. Constitution, the president is the commander in chief of the U.S. armed forces, while Congress is given the power to declare war. The Department of Defense conducts the day-to-day work of the military. The secretary of defense serves as a member of the president's cabinet.

Unquestionably, the U.S. military is the mightiest in the world. It benefits from superior training, outstanding technology, and ample funding. Key to its strength, however, is the strong base of men and women who serve their country bravely and with honor. By a wide margin, the United States ranks first in the world in military expenditures. The U.S. Navy and Air Force are the world's finest. Other nations, like China, have larger armies, but the U.S. Army possesses superior technology. Training and technology, not numbers alone, make the United States the world's leading military power.

This does not mean that the U.S. military and the country's citizens do not face challenges. They do! Threats posed by al Qaeda and the rising powers of China and Russia will continue to confront the United States in coming decades. That is why diplomacy conducted by the U.S. Department of State is vitally important. Hopefully, serious conflict or even war can be prevented through diplomatic means. Additionally, free trade between nations is building economic bridges that make military conflicts less likely. History also shows that democracies are less inclined to fight against each other. This means that diplomacy, the spread of democracy, and having a strong military are tools that can be used to reduce conflicts.

PRESENT-DAY PARTNERSHIPS

The United States has strategic partnerships with a number of allies. Key military defense partnerships include NATO, ANZUS, SEATO, and the Rio Pact. ANZUS stands for the Australia, New Zealand, United States Security Treaty, which was signed in 1951. ANZUS, like the NATO partnership, provides for the mutual defense of the nations that have signed the agreement. The United States has also signed a mutual defense agreement with Japan (1954) and the Southeast Asia Collective Defense Treaty (SEATO) with nine other nations (1954, disbanded in 1977). The United States also has a mutual defense agreement with countries in the Americas, called the Inter-American Treaty of Reciprocal Assistance (commonly called the Rio Pact). More than twenty countries in North and South America have signed the Rio Pact, which was ratified in 1947.

These strategic partnerships provide for assistance in the event any member is attacked. NATO has expanded in recent years. In 1999, former Soviet satellite nations Poland, Hungary, and the Czech Republic joined the group. Other former satellites, including Bulgaria, Estonia, Latvia, Lithuania, Slovakia, Slovenia, and Romania, joined in 2004. This brought the number of NATO members to 26. Also seeking membership in NATO are Croatia, Albania, Georgia, and the Ukraine. Some of these potential new members may be in conflict with the interests of Russia, which invaded the Republic of Georgia in 2008. Thus, the issue of NATO membership may serve as a source of future disagreements between the United States and Russia.

INTERNATIONAL ORGANIZATIONS

International organizations are very important in structuring the affairs of and relationships between countries. The largest of these is the United Nations (UN), with 192 member countries. The United States was a founding member in 1945. The UN has two major bodies. First is the General Assembly, in which all member nations participate. The second is the Security Council, which has 5 permanent members and 10 nonpermanent members who are elected by the General Assembly for two-year terms. The five permanent members are China, France, the Russian Federation, the United Kingdom, and the United States. Each council member has one vote, but the five permanent members have the power to veto measures. This means that measures can be opposed by any one of the permanent members and the veto will cause the item to fail.

The UN also has other affiliated bodies to which the United States belongs. They include the International Court of Justice (ICJ), the United Nations Children's Fund (UNICEF), and the World Health Organization (WHO). The bodies operating under the UN focus on more specific issues like health and justice. A complete listing of U.S. involvement in the United Nations can be found on the UN Web site.

The United States is also engaged in other organizations that serve regional or global interests or are linked by some common purpose or goal. Examples of regional organizations include the Arctic Council and the Organization of American States (OAS). Special issue groups are also often global and include organizations like the World Trade Organization (WTO), the World Customs Organization (WCO), or the International Energy Agency (IEA). More complete listings can be found at the U.S. State Department Web site or the CIA *World Factbook* Web site.

THE UNITED STATES AND THE UNITED NATIONS

The United States was a founding member of the United Nations when it was created right after World War II. The UN Charter was signed in San Francisco in 1945. Its headquarters is housed in the distinctive UN building in New York City. The United States is one of five permanent members of the UN Security Council. This position allows the United States to veto measures of the body if deemed necessary.

Even with all of these ties between the United States and the UN, the relationship has had its conflicts. Here are a few:

➡ With the fall of the Soviet Union, the United States became the world's only superpower. Thus, other nations would often unite though the UN to oppose U.S. power and hegemony. The body sometimes worked to limit unilateral activities of the United States.

➡ The United States has frequently vetoed measures that condemn Israel. This action is much to the dismay of Arab nations and others who believe that Israel has overreached its boundaries at times.

INTERNATIONAL AGREEMENTS

International agreements and treaties are another way that the United States participates in world affairs. These agreements are based upon shared principles that the countries signing the treaty agree to abide by. They serve a variety of purposes, from economic development to educational exchanges and nuclear nonproliferation. Sometimes these agreements are only between the United States and a single other country. Others may involve many countries.

The United States has signed onto a number of treaties and agreements. Many of these were signed in the eighteenth and

---

- ➔ The UN levies assessments upon countries as a way of getting funds for UN activities around the world. The United States has complained that the levy on the country was too high, and so Congress has not kept up with bills sent by the UN. The United States therefore is behind in what the UN has expected to receive in funds.
- ➔ The U.S. invasion of Iraq caused further conflict with the UN. Many countries believed that the United States did not have the approval of the UN to invade Iraq in 2003.

While the relationship between the United States and the UN is often one filled with disagreement, the United States has chosen to stay active in the world organization. The failure of the United States to participate in the League of Nations demonstrated that a world body was necessary to vent and discuss important issues. Thus, even with occasional disagreements, the United States remains an active member of the United Nations.

nineteenth centuries with Native American tribes, since they were sovereign peoples. Today's agreements and treaties are between countries. Examples of multinational agreements that involve the United States are the Nuclear Non-Proliferation Treaty (1968), the Outer Space Treaty (1967), the Antarctic Treaty (1961), and the Convention on Cybercrime (U.S. ratified in 2006). An

MAKING C⊕NNECTI⊕NS

GLOBAL AGREEMENTS AND YOUR LIFE

World treaties may appear to have little effect on our daily lives. However, when the documents are examined, the consequences of many agreements do actually affect our lives in a real and meaningful way. Examine the listed agreements and answer the questions that follow the list of treaties.

Agreements and Treaties
- North American Free Trade Agreement (NAFTA)
- Montreal Protocol on Substances That Deplete the Ozone Layer
- Inter-American Treaty of Reciprocal Assistance (Rio Pact)
- Universal Declaration of Human Rights
- Convention on the Rights of the Child

Questions
1. Does this agreement affect your life? If so, how?
2. Do you support the intent of the agreement?
3. How is the agreement working up to this point?
4. Do you believe the agreement has potential for success in achieving its objectives? Why or why not?
5. Can the agreement be improved? If so, how?

example of a bilateral agreement (between two countries) would be the Strategic Arms Reduction Treaty (START I) between the United States and Soviet Union (1991). Another would be the Treaty of Security between the United States and Japan that was signed in 1951 and updated in 1960.

The U.S. Constitution prescribes that the president provide leadership in treaty negotiations. The Constitution, however, requires ratification (approval) of all treaties by two-thirds of the Senate. Thus, a number of treaties negotiated by presidents have never been ratified. These include agreements such as the Treaty of Versailles (1919) ending World War I, the Comprehensive Test Ban Treaty (1996), and the Kyoto Protocol (2005) on climate change. On rare occasions, the United States has withdrawn from treaties as the politics change within the country. An example of this would be the Anti-Ballistic Missile Treaty. The United States signed on in 1972 but withdrew in 2002.

THE UNITED STATES AND GLOBAL ENVIRONMENTAL ISSUES

Environmental issues are increasingly the subject of international agreements. Weather patterns, pollution of the seas and rivers, air pollution, water usage, climate change, and other environmental issues impact more than one country. Thus, recent decades have seen increased efforts to safeguard the natural environment. Some of these issues, like climate change, are politically controversial in the United States. Thus, the country has signed and ratified some agreements like the Montreal Protocol (1989) on ozone layer depletion. But the United States has not signed or ratified the Kyoto Protocol (2005) on climate change.

PRESENT-DAY POLITICAL PROBLEMS

The United States, as the world's leading superpower, has assumed leadership in many world issues. U.S. presidents from Carter, to

Police investigate the scene of a suicide bombing in Tel Aviv, Israel, in 2006. Global terrorism is an issue in which the United States has become increasingly involved.

Clinton, to George W. Bush, to Barack Obama have attempted to bring peace to the Middle East, yet the quest continues. The lingering issue of global terrorism has spread the U.S. military to many locations around the world. Currently, the focus is on efforts to bring stability to Iraq and Afghanistan. Pakistan is a strategic nation, armed with nuclear weapons, that faces many internal challenges, including al Qaeda. Neighbors like Cuba and Venezuela have stuck like thorns in the side of U.S. influence in the Americas. Russia and China are rising in economic and military power. Oil imports and foreign purchases of U.S. businesses and treasury bills present new political problems.

Political issues confronting the United States are not solely international in scope. The 2008 presidential election showed a nation once again divided, as it was during the two preceding elections. The value of the dollar fell greatly in the first decade of the twenty-first century. A huge bailout of financial institutions was required in 2008 in order at least to attempt to mend problems within the country's economic system. Measures such as these forced the U.S. deficit up by another trillion dollars, to more than $10 trillion. Thus, even the world's most powerful nation continues to have political and economic problems at home and abroad.

U.S. HEGEMONY

Hegemony is an important word. Simply defined, it means control or a dominating influence over others. A school bully could have hegemony over many others at school. Why? Because of the power of the bully and the fear that other students feel. The same is true of international politics. The United States has hegemony over the Americas and even regions beyond because of its strong military and economic influence. The United States has frequently asserted its power and influence in the Americas and elsewhere. Other countries also work to assert their hegemony, as demonstrated clearly by Russia with its invasion of Georgia in 2008.

Hegemony is not necessarily a negative thing. The United States has often intervened in the affairs of other nations to protect their people and to provide stability. For example, in 1990, Iraq invaded Kuwait, its small southern neighbor. U.S. president George H.W. Bush built a coalition that freed Kuwait and contained Saddam Hussein's Iraqi forces. Under President Bill Clinton, the United States also used its influence and power to end ethnic cleansing and the war in Bosnia-Herzegovina in the 1990s. Thus hegemony can be positive or negative based on the way in which the stronger force exercises its power.

AMERICA'S SOCIAL AND CULTURAL ROLES

The United States is a world power in many ways, as earlier chapters have spotlighted. But the country is also a world leader in one way that, at first, may seem frivolous. It is an important role that carries multiple influences beyond the borders of the country. Sometimes these influences are welcomed and sometimes they are resented and rejected.

U.S. POPULAR CULTURE

U.S. popular culture is exported around the world in many ways. American music, art, and literature have spread worldwide, as have movies, television programs, and even sports. When traveling around the world, it is very common to hear songs by Britney Spears, Justin Timberlake, Jay-Z, Outkast, Madonna, Rihanna, and many others. U.S. television programs, sporting events, and movies appear around the world, often dubbed or subtitled in the local language. Thus, when an American leaves the country, he or she still comes in frequent contact with U.S. popular culture.

All of these elements carry U.S. culture around the world. A new song can become a global hit overnight because of the Internet and global communications systems. Athletic achievements also spread at the same speed. U.S. sports heroes, singers, and other celebrities become global stars. The United States has become a factory of popular culture, and its products are a major export.

U.S. POPULAR CULTURE AND THE WORLD

The speed and quality of communications and transportation systems has helped to facilitate the United States' role as a major cultural powerhouse. In decades past, films and videotapes would be sent overseas with later releases than in the United States. Today, films are released concurrently in multiple locations around the world. This is happening as communication and transportation systems move movies, music, sports, and television programs almost immediately via satellites and the Internet. As an example, just a few years ago, records and tapes needed to be made and sent to transmit music around the world. Today, people simply download their favorite songs. Movies and television programs are available in the same manner.

Another area of U.S. popular culture is the handheld media and communications technology that is available today. From iPods and iPhones to BlackBerrys and laptop computers, information and entertainment are now immediately available. U.S. technology is another cultural export, with Google, Apple, Yahoo!, Microsoft, and others reaching around the planet with their technology and applications. Popular Web sites like You-Tube, Second Life, Facebook, and MySpace further disseminate U.S. culture. The speed at which information and cultural elements now flow out from the United States has reached an unprecedented pace.

Television programs are further evidence of the United States' cultural reach. From *Baywatch* to *Desperate Housewives*, programs are followed as enthusiastically overseas as they are in the United States. Many also use the programs as a device for learning English, the international language of business, science, and culture. Even television game shows take on local variations as they spread from the United States and the United Kingdom to other places. For example, *Jeopardy!* started in the United States in 1954 but is now mimicked in New Zealand, Germany, France, Russia, Argentina, Sweden, Israel, Turkey, and other countries. *Dancing with the Stars* was developed in the United Kingdom but gained international fame in the United States. Now the reality series has local variations in Australia, Brazil, Bulgaria, Peru, South Africa, and other countries. Many other programs fall into the pattern of being filmed in the United States and distributed around the world. In addition to teaching language, the programs also portray, often inaccurately, what many people overseas believe is typical American life.

AMERICAN TELEVISION

The United States is a television hub that churns out programs that are syndicated and broadcast around the world. Distribution companies work to sell programs to at least one major station in other countries to extend their profits. Thus, a variety of television programs are syndicated, including reality programs, sports, talk shows, and game shows. Nations where English is spoken are often easier markets than countries where other languages are spoken. These countries will still broadcast many syndicated programs by having native speakers voice the words of the American programs in their home language.

In addition to syndicated programs, CNN broadcasts news around the world via satellite. However, the international news feed is different than the CNN broadcast in the United States.

A Chinese student watches a dubbed version of an American television program. U.S. popular culture is so far-reaching that American movies, music, books, and TV shows are available in even the most unlikely places.

Billions of dollars are earned by U.S. interests because of the movies, television programs, music, and sports that are exported worldwide. Movies alone will bring in an estimated $42 billion annually by early 2012. These cultural revenues represent a significant export for the country, but they are threatened by illegal copying and sharing of songs, movies, programs, and events. Stolen satellite signals and streaming video steal further revenue. Piracy is estimated to cost the industry about $20 billion each year, and the problem is increasing. Illegal copies of movies and CDs are found in markets in China, Malaysia, and in many other countries, including the United States itself.

THE UNITED STATES IN WORLD SPORTS

The United States is also a recognized leader in the world in sports. Many of these sports, like lacrosse, a game of early Native Americans, were invented in the United States. Others invented in the United States include windsurfing, volleyball, Ultimate Frisbee, softball, paintball, beach volleyball, and hacky sack. Some of the inventions are readily visible, like basketball, which was invented in the United States by a Canadian, James Naismith.

Many of these sports have become popular around the world in professional leagues like the National Basketball Association (NBA). Stars like Bryant, O'Neal, and James are immediately recognized around the world as Kobe, Shaq, and Lebron. This has happened as NBA games are carried live on television via satellite or over the Internet for wide viewing. NBA jerseys and T-shirts are seen in places like Nigeria, Australia, and Serbia since teams have fans around the world. In addition, the NBA has become an international league with players from countries around the world. These include players from China, Germany, Argentina, Brazil, Croatia, Canada, Australia, Senegal, Spain, Russia, Ukraine, Italy, Serbia, France, and Slovenia. To appeal to its wide fan base, the NBA Web site is offered in many languages, including French, Spanish, Portuguese, Chinese, Korean, German, Italian, and Japanese.

Traditional sports aren't the only sports exported from the United States. New sports, like the Ultimate Fighting Championship (UFC), are becoming increasingly popular overseas after the seeds were first planted in the United States. The UFC is for fighters who use mixed martial arts in their sport. The UFC has spread quickly in the twenty-first century, and it is now watched in 35 countries with the number expanding rapidly. The winter and summer X Games have also become international.

While sports like basketball and hockey are taken seriously, others fall into the category of entertainment. Nonetheless, they

In Tokyo, Japan, U.S. basketball star Kobe Bryant holds a clinic for area youth. Bryant and other sports stars are so popular around the globe that they embark on world tours to reach all of their fans.

are immensely popular overseas. First among these is professional wrestling. With colorful personalities and story lines, the World Wrestling Entertainment, Inc. (WWE) is a global sports entertainment company. The WWE claims to be showing its programs in 110 countries as fans around the world enjoy this form of sports entertainment.

OTHER INFLUENCES

American cultural influences also come in other forms. They range from comic strips such as *Garfield* and *Peanuts* to satellite

MAKING C●NNECTI●NS

GLOBAL MUSIC

Music has become a major connection between countries in the age of the Internet. Thus, entertainers like Madonna, from Michigan; Britney Spears, from Louisiana; or Curtis James Jackson III (better known as rapper 50 Cent), from New York, can quickly spread their music and videos around the world. Use the Internet and other information to research the following questions to determine the popularity of American musicians around the world.

- List three of your favorite American musicians or musical groups.
- Identify two or three of the most popular songs these musicians have recorded.
- Determine how they have disseminated their music. (e.g., iTunes, compact discs).
- Determine places in the world outside of the United States where these songs and entertainers are popular.
- Identify some of the places these musicians entertained when touring abroad.

radio programs. American fast foods have swept across the world so that a visitor to Barcelona, Beijing, Kuala Lumpur, or Paris can have a fast-food feast at McDonald's, KFC, or Pizza Hut. Coca-Cola and Pepsi-Cola are also worldwide ventures with advertisements that carry U.S. interests overseas. Other U.S. businesses carry their corporate culture and the English language with them when working in other countries. All of these commercial activities are spreading U.S. practices and culture to other countries.

The U.S. government has cultural programs overseas that assist people in understanding the United States. These include libraries and displays that feature American art, history, and even tragedies like September 11, 2001. The purpose of these efforts is to help other nations understand the United States better. Through understanding, they may be more sympathetic to the United States. Some critics see these displays as being propaganda. Others see them as efforts to promote democracy and freedom. The Voice of America is a major effort by the United States to counter propaganda. It broadcasts in nearly 50 languages around the world. It even has an effort in the Middle East aimed at young people. Called Radio Sawa, it broadcasts American popular music. These international broadcasts are also available over the Internet using servers in more than 70 countries.

The State Department sponsors a number of cultural exchange programs that allow foreigners to observe the United States more closely. These exchanges are offered to students, journalists, and scholars. Managers, entertainers, and others also are eligible to receive financial assistance to travel to and study in the United States. Not only are the grants for people overseas, but they are also available for Americans who hope to travel and study overseas. Application can be made through the Fulbright Program, which is sponsored by the U.S. Department of State.

The United States is an incredibly complex country culturally. This reality makes it impossible to list all of the country's global cultural influences. The spread of U.S. culture is generally welcomed internationally. But there are those who vehemently object to it. For example, the societal roles of U.S. women as portrayed in movies and television is often rejected by nations with conservative religious values like Saudi Arabia. Some of the U.S. media are also rejected by nations like Singapore. That small island country is critical of U.S. reporting of its political, social, and economic conditions. Thus, while many enjoy U.S. culture and work to learn English, many others resent the intrusion of this foreign culture on their traditional values and beliefs.

AMERICA'S FUTURE ROLES IN THE WORLD

At the end of the first decade of the twenty-first century, Americans pondered their future. Economic markets were in turmoil. There was deep concern over possible terrorism. The country was involved militarily in Afghanistan and Iraq. Both the U.S. and world economies were in shambles. Many Americans feared for their jobs and for their investments, including retirement programs. The 2008 election promised change, but Americans seemed uncertain and unsteady in their belief of a better future. The United States' role in the world was changing—but toward what?

INTRODUCTION OF FUTURES PERSPECTIVES

Since the future is always unknown, futurists present three different ways of thinking about times ahead. They suggest examining the probable, possible, and preferred futures. What do these mean?

The probable future would be the one that is a logical result of what history has led us to now. It examines what the natural progression from this point in time would be if we follow the same path.

Possible futures cast a wider net. They examine a wide a range of futures that include many important variables. For example, what if there is a major national expenditure on alternative energy? This could create a possible future that relies less on the Middle East and unstable governments that possess oil. However, the world could end up fighting a major war over dwindling oil supplies. Possible futures can include many variables like climate change, a faltering world economy, technological breakthroughs, population growth, and numerous other considerations.

Preferred futures are perhaps the most hopeful. This view is shaped by policies that will create a "preferred" future. Undoubtedly, this is what humankind wants to do. But conflicting political views on public policy cloud the creation of the preferred future. For example, the major political parties in the United States differ on how a better economic future can be attained. One view believes strongly in a free market system with little government interference. The other view holds that government must regulate the marketplace to maintain fairness. It also believes in greater government involvement in the economy. Each group believes strongly that its policies will lead to the preferred future. Which of these actually will lead to the best future is unclear. Only time will tell.

The following sections examine selected issues facing the United States and its future roles in the world. We will use the tools that have been presented to examine the possible, probable, and preferred futures.

ECONOMIC FUTURES

The U.S. and global economic systems teetered precariously on the edge of collapse in late 2008. Demand for energy had even dropped as the world's stock markets crashed. This economic impact is perhaps hardest to forecast since the turmoil hadn't totally settled by the end of the year. Nonetheless, some things are foreseeable, since many energy sources use oil, coal, natural gas, and other limited resources. Their continued use will encourage a search for additional sources, which will be more expensive to produce. This and rising demand will increase prices. Alternative energy strategies have potential, but the mass production of solar, tidal, and wind energy has remained mostly only a promise. By the end of the first decade of the twenty-first century, renewable sources generated only a small portion of the United States' and the world's energy needs.

Competition from around the world, including cheaper labor in places like India and China, has changed the nature of U.S. industry. However, the know-how and can-do attitude of the United States' productive labor force continues to shape the future. Creative ideas born on U.S. soil seem to work their way into the global marketplace, leaving the probable future much like the past. However, quality education remains an important key to the United States' success in this area. Today, both India and China are educating many more engineers and scientists than is the United States. The gap may be filled by immigrants who bring their education and talents into the United States' labor force as they have in the past.

A major concern will be the enormous debt that the U.S. government continues to accumulate. After the 2008 economic crisis in housing and banking, the U.S. deficit grew to more than $10 trillion. This is a number so high that the U.S. National Debt Clock in New York City ran out of digits on October 8, 2008. This debt means that a significant amount of money is paid in interest and cannot be used for other purposes. It also holds some unknown consequences, because much of the debt is owned by foreign countries like Japan and China. Another potential consequence is the falling value of the dollar as demand for the currency falls around the world.

Ultimately, future economic challenges will fall back onto the shoulders of the United States' workforce and leadership in both the public and private sectors. The free market structure has long been held as important, but the horrendous economic circumstances in 2008 caused both political parties to support greater government involvement in private industries. This development may change the future possibilities in ways that cannot be easily anticipated.

POLITICAL FUTURES

The election of 2008 brought back some of the United States' divisions. Some were the same as recent elections with the red states (Republican Party) and blue states (Democratic Party) division. Others reopened old divisions based on gender and race. With the presidential candidacy of Senator Hillary Clinton and the vice presidential candidacy of Governor Sarah Palin, women were contending for the highest offices in the country. This brought out issues that were new to the political arena. At the same time, Senator Barack Obama, half African American and half Anglo American, brought back questions of race with his unprecedented candidacy. Senator John McCain brought the issue of ageism back to political discussions.

MAKING CONNECTIONS

HOW IS THE UNITED STATES CHANGING TODAY?

What important issues dominate newspaper headlines and the electronic media in the United States today? What are the major viewpoints on how to resolve these issues? What do you think should be done and why?

Thus, the 2008 presidential election featured gender, race, and age issues along with an economic crisis, the War on Terror, and other normal political discussions. Both presidential candidates, Obama and McCain, promised change, a direction that voters seemed ready to embrace. While the election campaigns advanced with rhetoric and accusations from both sides, the U.S. government kept working.

A feature of the U.S. government that is underappreciated is the calm transition of government from one ruling party and president to the next. While other nations may have elections marked by violence and assassinations, Americans have accepted the results of elections—even when close. This was clearly demonstrated in the unusual presidential election of 2000. Then vice president Al Gore received more actual (popular) votes than did incoming president George W. Bush. But Bush received the most electoral votes. Even with court cases and controversy, the country calmly accepted the decision of the U.S. Supreme Court in *Bush v. Gore*. This political tradition and others have helped to make the United States a safe haven for foreign investors and a destination for immigrants from around the world.

Thus, while the election of 2008 was hotly contested, the election of Barack Obama was quickly accepted by Americans. After elections, the United States moves forward under the leadership of new presidents to continue to tackle the nation's challenges.

SOCIAL AND CULTURAL FUTURES

The social and cultural treasures created in the United States will also most likely continue to impress the world. New movies produced in Hollywood quickly become global hits. Television programs and music created in the United States also quickly sweep across the world. The X Games and Ultimate Fighting have joined international staples like World Wrestling Entertainment in entertaining people. New information systems provided by the Internet and satellite communications continue to broadcast and narrowcast (transmission to only a select audience, like a cable system) U.S. entertainment overseas. Few see U.S. creative energy declining in the future.

ENVIRONMENTAL FUTURES

Americans have become increasingly concerned about the environment. Issues like climate change, pollution, and ozone depletion are increasingly embraced. What will this mean? These factors have already led to increased efforts to assist in creating positive environmental change. Some of these actions by citizens have led to laws protecting the environment. Others have led to greater personal responsibility for the environment. Personal actions include recycling and using energy-efficient appliances and cars.

Many political leaders are advocating that the United States become a leader in developing new energies and protecting the environment at the same time. Thus, clean solar, wind, and tidal energy production has captured the attention of citizens and their leaders. U.S. political leaders stress that these new sources of energy can create new jobs. While the future of many global environmental issues is unclear, Americans and their government are starting to take action. Both political parties in the 2008 election were much more concerned about these issues than they had been in the past. All of these trends indicate that the environmental future in the United States may be set to improve.

A NATION UNITED OR DIVIDED?

One major question remains for Americans as they move further into the twenty-first century. Will they unite to tackle the important challenges ahead of them? Divisions have torn apart the political fabric of the United States in recent decades. Both political parties and their followers are responsible. Issues of race, gender, sexuality, war, the environment, terrorists, and the economy cast dark clouds over the country. Can the United States really afford to be so divided at a time of peril?

COMMENTS ABOUT THE UNITED STATES FROM THE WORLD

Many people around the world are vocal about their views of the United States. The range of views is very diverse. Here is a sampling of views from overseas:

"America is a large, friendly dog in a very small room. Every time it wags its tail, it knocks over a chair." —*Arnold Toynbee, English philosopher and historian*

"You can always count on Americans to do the right thing—after they've tried everything else." —*Winston Churchill, British prime minister*

"What the United States does best is to understand itself. What it does worst is understand others." —*Carlos Fuentes, Mexican writer*

"Russians can give you arms but only the United States can give you a solution." —*Anwar el-Sādāt, third Egyptian president*

Here are a few observations about their country made by U.S. presidents:

"I still believe in a place called Hope, a place called America." —*William J. Clinton, forty-second U.S. president*

"Our nation is the enduring dream of every immigrant who ever set foot on these shores, and the millions still struggling to be free. This nation, this idea called America, was and always will be a new world—our new world." —*George H.W. Bush, forty-first U.S. president*

"America is too great for small dreams." —*Ronald Reagan, fortieth U.S. president*

"The wisest use of American strength is to advance freedom." —*George W. Bush, forty-third U.S. president*

"There is nothing wrong with America that cannot be cured with what is right in America." —*William J. Clinton, forty-second U.S. president*

After the violent terrorist attacks on the United States on September 11, 2001, the country came together for a few months. Both political parties stood together and were united against the people who had attacked the country. It was a time like few others in U.S. history when all stood together regardless of race, gender, religion, or political belief. Perhaps this kind of unity is the greatest asset in the United States' unknown future. On the other hand, continued fragmentation is perhaps the country's greatest threat. Whether Americans stride into the future united or sharply divided is a major issue that future leaders must address. As Americans have long said, "United we stand, divided we fall." The future will provide them with many tests. Few great civilizations have lasted more than a few centuries. How much longer does the United States have at the top?

A FINAL LOOK

The twentieth century ended with the United States as the world's only superpower. How will the United States fare in the twenty-first century? History suggests that the future will most likely have the United States continuing as a world power. While it may not fall in this century, others may continue to rise. Thus, even with the United States remaining a world superpower, others may also become superpowers. These will likely include countries like China, Russia, and India.

The United States does not necessarily need to fall to have these countries rise. Their economic growth may simply rise faster than that of the United States. Thus, the future may be multipolar, with a number of superpowers instead of just one or two. Nuclear proliferation also provides a wild card as more nations seek to possess this powerful weapon. As you have seen, the future of the United States is bright with opportunities, but danger and risks also lurk along the pathway to the future. Clearly, the continued vigilance, creativity, participation, education, labor, and energy of U.S. citizens remain the most important foundation for the United States' future.

GLOSSARY

annex   To take over a territory and incorporate the lands into another political entity.

capitalism   A free-market economic system where property is owned privately and profit is a motive for business ventures.

diplomacy   Negotiation between nations.

draft   A system of ordering citizens to report for military service.

entrepreneur   A person who starts or finances new business ventures.

ethnic cleansing   The forced and systematic removal of an ethnic group from its home area by any means.

gross domestic product (GDP)   The total value of goods and services produced in a country.

hegemony   The control or influence a powerful country has over other countries because of its economic, political, or military strength.

human rights   The rights and freedoms that all people are entitled to simply because they are human.

imperialism   A belief in creating empires that possess colonies around the world for economic, political, cultural, and military purposes.

indigenous   The original people living in a specific region.

isolationist   A government policy that avoids political and economic ties with other countries in the belief that national interests are better served.

Manifest Destiny   The nineteenth-century American belief that the country had a destiny of stretching from the Atlantic Ocean to the Pacific Ocean and beyond.

Monroe Doctrine   A policy issued by President James Monroe stating that foreign powers were not welcome to colonize or interfere with the new countries in the Americas.

North Atlantic Treaty Organization (NATO)   A defense organization formed in 1949 that includes the United States and allies who will respond if any members are attacked.

Open Door Policy   A U.S. policy that required China to provide equal trading opportunities to all countries.

puppet government   A government that is actually directed and controlled by an outside authority.

transparency   Openness in government.

veto   The power to reject legislation.

BIBLIOGRAPHY

Albright, Madeleine. *The Mighty and the Almighty: Reflections on America, God, and World Affairs*. New York: Harper Perennial, 2007.

Friedman, Thomas L. *The World Is Flat 3.0: A Brief History of the Twenty-first Century*. New York: Picador, 2007.

Gray, Colin S. *The Sheriff: America's Defense of the New World Order*. Lexington: University Press of Kentucky, 2004.

Herring, George C. *From Colony to Superpower: U.S. Foreign Relations Since 1776*. New York: Oxford University Press, 2008.

Kohut, Andrew, and Bruce Stokes. *America Against the World: How We Are Different and Why We Are Disliked*. New York: Holt Paperbacks, 2007.

Mandelbaum, Michael. *The Case for Goliath: How America Acts as the World's Government in the Twenty-first Century*. New York: Public Affairs, 2005.

Root, Hilton L. *Alliance Curse: How America Lost the Third World*. Washington, DC: Brookings Institution Press, 2008.

Serewicz, Lawrence W. *America at the Brink of Empire: Rusk, Kissinger, and the Vietnam War*. Baton Rouge: Louisiana State University Press, 2007.

Zakaria, Fareed. *The Post-American World*. New York: W.W. Norton & Company, 2008.

FURTHER RESOURCES

Bernstein, Vivian. *America's Story: Book One, to 1865*. Austin, TX: Harcourt, 2005.

Bernstein, Vivian. *America's Story: Book Two, Since 1865*. Austin, TX: Harcourt, 2005.

Dudley, William, ed. *Opposing Viewpoints in American History: From Reconstruction to the Present*. Farmington Hills, MI: Greenhaven Press, 2006.

Garcia, Jesus. *Creating America: A History of the United States*. Boston: Houghton Mifflin, 2006.

Gerdes Louise I., ed. *How Safe Is America's Infrastructure?* Detroit: Greenhaven Press, 2009.

Nakaya, Andrea C. *America in the Twenty-first Century*. Farmington Hills, MI: Greenhaven Press, 2006.

Papp, Daniel S., Lock K. Johnson, and John E. Endicott. *American Foreign Policy: History, Politics, and Policy*. New York: Pearson Longman, 2005.

Zinn, Howard, and Rebecca Stefoff, adaptor. *A Young People's History of the United States: Class Struggle to the War on Terror*. (Vol. 2). New York: Seven Stories Press, 2009.

WEB SITES

About.Com

http://americanhistory.about.com/

Site offers various U.S. history time periods and other useful information about the United States.

America's Library

http://www.americaslibrary.gov/cgi-bin/page.cgi/jb

Library of Congress site for youth on American history.

CIA *World Factbook*

https://www.cia.gov/library/publications/the-world-factbook/

Site provided by the U.S. Central Intelligence Agency with country briefs that provide detailed information on the United States and other countries.

North Atlantic Treaty Organization

http://www.nato.int/

Home site for NATO. Provides information on the organization and its members.

United Nations

http://www.un.org/

Site provides information on UN documents, related organizations, member countries (including the United States), human rights, and international data.

United States Department of State

http://www.state.gov/

Provides an overview of the U.S. Department of State, current issues, countries of the world, press releases, strategic plans, State Department careers, etc.

PICTURE CREDITS

INDEX

ABOUT THE AUTHOR

DOUGLAS A. PHILLIPS is an educator, writer, and consultant who has worked and traveled in more than 100 countries on 6 continents. From Alaska to Argentina and from Madagascar to Mongolia, he has worked as a middle school teacher, administrator, curriculum developer, author, and trainer of educators. Phillips has served as the president of the National Council for Geographic Education and has received the Outstanding Service Award from the National Council for the Social Studies along with numerous other awards. He serves as a senior consultant for the Center for Civic Education. Phillips lives with his family in Arizona.

ABOUT THE EDITOR

CHARLES F. GRITZNER holds the title distinguished professor of geography at South Dakota State University in Brookings. He is now in his fifth decade of college teaching and research. In addition to teaching, he enjoys travel, writing, working with teachers, and sharing his love for geography with young people. As a senior consulting editor and frequent author for Chelsea House Publishers' MODERN WORLD NATIONS, MODERN WORLD CULTURES, EXTREME ENVIRONMENTS, and GLOBAL CONNECTIONS series, he has a wonderful opportunity to combine each of these "hobbies." Dr. Gritzner has served as both president and executive director of the National Council for Geographic Education and has received the council's highest honor, the George J. Miller award for distinguished service to geographic education, as well as other honors from the NCGE, the Association of American Geographers, and other organizations.